THE COM BREVILLE SMART AIR FRYER OVEN PRO COOKBOOK WITH PICTURES

Healthy, Effortless & Mouthwatering Air Fryer Oven Recipes

for

Beginners and Advanced Users

Emma R. LeBlanc

TABLE OF CONTENTS

INTRODUCTION

The Breville Smart Air Fryer is an appliance that can replace a deep fryer, microwave, and oven in your kitchen, as well as allow you to cook in it.

The Breville Smart Air Fryer is a kitchen appliance that cooks food in a special chamber using super-heated air. The hot air in the cooking chamber is heated by the convection mechanism, which cooks your food evenly from all sides. The Maillard reaction gives fried food its distinctive flavor. Thanks to the hot air, your food gets a moist interior and doesn't taste like fat.

Because it's a healthier way to fry! It all depends on health, speed, and Versatility, so my answer is always the same. If it's done, you can "set it and forget it". No one needs to keep an eye on it. You can walk away from the oven without worrying about overcooked or burned food. An air fryer cooks your food evenly because it uses constant heat. It is energy-efficient and space-saving.

The air fryers cook food with hot air in the air. It's what you put into them that makes them so hard to eat. The Maillard Effect makes it possible to cook food quickly without losing the nutrients and flavor.

Please leave a review for this book if you find it helpful.

You can easily guess why the Breville Smart Oven Air Fryer Pro is one of the most popular electric ovens on the market today. It is possible to cook everything from French fries and chicken to cheese fries and deep-fried treats using high heat air. And guess what happens? You don't need any oil to use this product.

My experience with the Breville Smart Oven Air Fryer Pro has been so beneficial that I will share some basic tips and tricks. Here are some things you have to do to stay safe. It's best if you learn how to use the Breville Smart Oven Air Fryer Pro before you buy it. This book will help you learn how to use your oven so that your meals will be delicious.

The Breville Smart Oven Air Fryer Pro comes with a high-tech and well-known technology called the Element IQ technology. This large countertop oven is great for you if you want to prepare a lot of fries for a large group. French fries are so good, they don't leave a mess on your fingers and forearms. The different controls on this device have contributed to making Breville the toast of many users worldwide.

The unit comes with a choice of two temperature controls and an intelligent navigation system, which I discovered after purchasing it. This food thermometer uses a color-coded ring to show you the temperature of the food. You can also find a screen on the front of the oven that displays the time, temperature, and other settings.

The oven's design is clear, and I found up to 10 different ways to cook. It is a level of sophistication and flexibility I have to experience. The Breville Smart Oven Air Fryer Pro is my favorite new addition to my kitchen.

THE BREVILLE SMART OVEN AIR FRYER PRO HAS THESE FEATURES

Since purchasing the Breville Smart Oven Air Fryer Pro, I enjoy cooking more because of the many unique features that allow easy use. Breville is a popular appliance among home cooks, chefs, and kitchen workers.

- The Breville Smart Oven Air Fryer Pro uses the Element IQ Technology to cook food faster and better by directing the power to where it is most needed inside the oven. It contains an internal algorithm for controlling the six-quartz heat-generating elements for cooking, and uses heat sensors and temperature control elements to detect and cancel cold parts.

You can choose your own cooking settings. Your personalized settings will be saved even when the oven is unplugged from the power source.

- I effectively cook chicken wings, French fries, and many more air fried foods with this setting. Breville uses a blend of higher temperature and super convection to make its air fryer. The function of the oven makes air fryers obsolete.
- Dual Speed Convection: This technology cooks food faster. The new dual-speed convection oven cooks food 30% faster than my old one. A lot of my other activities have been saved by it. It's good for many cooking techniques, including air frying, dehydrating, proofing and roasting.
- LCD: The LCD screen on the Breville Smart Oven Air Fryer Pro makes it easier to use the device's many functions, adjust a wide range of settings, and cook food with more freedom and control. My command center for all my cooking activities is helped by it because it helps me know when different cooking techniques are completed.
- When opening the oven door and cooking, the smart lighting system within the oven will turn on automatically. The light illuminates the inside of the oven during a cooking cycle.
- It has a large capacity to fit a large turkey, a large Dutch oven, and a lot of other things. It's a big oven. I use it for cooking and spend less time in the kitchen. With a Breville Smart Oven Air Fryer Pro, you may not need to purchase another oven.
- Accessories and warranty: The Smart Oven Air Fryer Pro comes with extra accessories like pizza stones, pizza crisper pans, and bamboo cutting boards. There are more air fry baskets, roasting pans, wire racks, and broiling Racks. The oven comes with a 2-year limited warranty. If you have any issues with your purchase, you can take it to an approved store and get it fixed.
- Versatile: If you're looking for an all-in-one cooking station, you've found one in Breville Smart Oven Air Fryer Pro. The aim is to give you the best cooking experience every time, with 13 functions put into one big machine. It is possible to cook for a long time at any temperature and time setting.

THE FUNCTIONS OF THE BREVILLE SMART AIR FRYER OVEN PRO

As you will discover the following functions, they are even more enjoyable to explore.

- Toast Function: With this, you can adjust the level of darkness you want to achieve with certain food items and the number of slices you want to toast. The cooking time automatically changes depending on the number of slices. When I cook bread, English muffins, and waffles, I usually use the time dial to change the cooking duration, but you can also manually do it.
- Bagel function: This function requires no preheat cycle. I liked using this for my bagel. To use, I cut my bagel, put it in the oven, and set the oven to Bagel function. This setting helps to crisp the insides of my bagels while I toast them.
- Broil Function: Thin slices of meat, sandwiches, poultry products, fish, and vegetables are good for broiling. I also use it to make sausages, desserts, casseroles, and gratins. Air and heat are evenly distributed around the food you're cooking.
- Bake Function: The bake function uses all six of the heating elements in a smart way, and I found it useful for cakes, brownies, and muffins. It is possible to place your food in the oven after preheating.
- Roast Function: The roast function gives me the taste of a barbeque, right in my kitchen. Convection settings are also used in roasting. You can adjust the settings during the roasting cycle.

- Pizza Function: This function is designed to get the best out of every pizza you eat. You need to preheat your oven before using a pizza pan or stone.
- Proof Function: This cooking technique uses a proof function to evenly distribute low temperatures around the oven. Pizza, dough, breads, rolls and other foods can be proofed with this. I put dough in an oven-proof container and cover it, placing it at the center of the oven. It's possible to leave my food for as long as 2 hours with the Smart Oven's automatic cooking function.
- Air Fry Function: The Breville Smart Oven Air Fryer has an Air Fry function. Many technologies are used to produce well-cooked, crisp and brown foods in the oven. I use this function for a lot of different things. The Air Fry function combines the heating power of the quartz elements with the smart heat control and airflow systems to produce satisfying results.
- Cookies Function: Cookies are a kind of food that can be prepared by baking. It was useful for cookies and small cupcakes. To bake your food to perfection, you need to preheat your oven and use the convection settings.
- Dehydrate Function: A huge plus for many owners is the availability of thehydrate function on the Breville Smart Oven Air Fryer. The oven has a built-in fan for efficient airflow, which helps to dry food items faster and more evenly. I really like the fact that I can choose how long I leave my food in the oven without it burning or overcooking.
- Slow Cook Function: The Slow Cook Function is useful for cooking food over long periods of time at lower temperatures. This helps me a lot when I want to take a nap or do something else while cooking. You can set your oven to preheat, choose the right temperature and time, and then turn your attention to something else.
- Reheat Function: It can be very tedious to prepare different dishes for guests. It gets worse when it gets cold so quickly and you're tired. It's not a problem anymore, as the reheat function is great for leftover food that gets cold.
- Warm Function: It's one of the best things I could ever ask for, and the oven's warm function gives me just this, after a long day at work. What more could we ask for than a single appliance that could warm our meals as well? Use the Warm function for leftover meals and those that have cooled off.

THE CONTROL PANEL

With a powerful control center and different knobs, the Breville Smart Oven Air Fryer Pro is able to give you the most engaging cooking experience possible. The control panel is located on the right edge of the oven, and it has a few buttons and knobs.

- An interactive LCD: As the world changes, I have to be more dynamic with my kitchen choices, and I believe the same goes for you. The Breville Smart Oven Air Fryer Pro has a Crystal Display that is important to me. The LCD screen on the Smart Oven Air Fryer Pro is a command center for all the machine's functions. This oven gives you a view into the details of how your food is cooking.
- The temperature control knob lets you set how much heat is on your food. If you want to cook with toast darkness levels, the temperature knob is the way to go.
- You can change the temperature unit by pressing a button. You can also use this button to change the sound produced by your oven.
- The Start button is what you will use to start the cooking cycle. When the cooking is done, you can manually end the cooking cycle.
- Time knob: For most cooking techniques, the knob helps you select the cooking duration. You can use the time dial for selections when using the Toast functions.
- You can turn on the oven lights when you open the oven door. You can turn the oven lights on or off at any time during a cooking cycle.
- The button helps you choose the settings that are suitable for the meal you want to cook.

BENEFITS OF USING THE BREVILLE SMART OVEN AIR FRYER PRO

Since using the Breville Smart Oven Air Fryer Pro, I have enjoyed many benefits. You will be able to confirm this claim if you own one. The ingenious way in which a single appliance incorporates so many functions is still a technological marvel. I find the Breville Smart Oven Air Fryer Pro very attractive because it helps me get the optimal levels of productivity every day.

- It has a lot of space, which is great for large cooking dinners. With the oven air fryer, I have been able to make use of all of the functions and get wonderful results with my recipes.
- It is impressive that the rack and baskets are made of good quality steel.
- The time I cook has been reduced by about 30%, just as was stated in the package. This is because of the super convection setting that helps make French fries crispier and other dishes that require dehydration.
- My bread can be made in the exact way I want it. Your bread will be finished to exactness if you choose how brown you want it to be.

- The Smart Oven Air Fryer Pro has the perfect pans for my oven. This saves you from having to buy these special cooking containers.
- It's possible to choose from a variety of colors for the Breville Smart Oven Air Fryer Pro.

HOW TO USE THE BREVILLE SMART AIR FRYER OVEN

Your air fryer is very easy to use. You can get going with the following steps.

1. The power cord of the Breville Smart Air Fryer Oven can be hazardous if it is not in good shape, so it is important to check the components first.
2. The air fryer oven needs to be removed. A grounded power outlet is where you should put it. Plug the air fryer oven.
3. Take out the baking trays from the oven. Right after unboxing the oven, wash all removable parts with a clean cloth before use.
4. To use the time button, set the oven to PIZZA.
5. You must press the start button to finish the cooking cycle. Your Breville Smart Oven is now ready for use.

TIPS AND PRECAUTIONS

The Breville Smart Oven Air Fryer Pro is a great way to cook several things at once. A technology-driven air fryer is one of the appliances in one appliance. Baking a few cupcakes and muffins was very enjoyable. I toast a few slices of bread, which I did not regret. The first time I did with my oven air fryer pro, I made large 8-inch cakes and chocolate chip cookies. I now use the microwave for most of my cooking. The air fryer oven is easy to use and fun to use, especially after finding the right recipe.Here are some things that helped me after using the Breville Smart Oven Air Fryer Pro for a few months:

- If you are using the slow cook function, place a lid on the cookware.
- Cut the chicken into smaller pieces before cooking. It allows the food to be uniformly cooked.
- It is not advisable to fill cookware to the brim. Keeping the contents to half their capacity will help you avoid spills.
- Choose a lighter set of cookware that can go in the oven.
- Don't leave oil on the grill or in your fryer for long.
- If you have a power outlet that is unstable, don't use an appliance.

There are a couple of things to be aware of while handling the Breville Smart Oven Air Fryer Pro. I came up with a list of precautions to take when using the oven after running into a few troubles.

- It's important that you use the grilling rack inside the roasting pan if your recipe features food that drips grease or oil.
- Don't forget to remove the oven from the power outlet before cleaning it out.
- The oven air fryer should be handled with care around children. The metallic parts could be very hot. I usually leave the oven to cool for at least half an hour before I disassemble the parts for cleaning. You can save yourself from pain by using it, but it also helps to preserve the air fry baskets and the rack.
- To clean the heating element, I use a soft sponge to gently rub along the length. This is a habit that you should keep up. It's better to ignore the standard oven cleaner because it makes the metal surface of the interior degrade quicker. Oven cleaners contain non-abrasive sponges and non-corrosive cleaning liquid soaps. This way you can clean your oven while extending its life.
- It's important that you put the crumb tray into the oven and place the broiling rack into the roasting pan. If you leave it to rest on the wire rack, it will be safer.
- When you are not using the Breville Smart Oven Air Fryer Pro, make sure it is dry. I have learned to keep the oven door closed so that the interior heating system is not disrupted.
- Always keep your Smart Oven Air Fryer Pro upright, for all it's worth. The top of the oven is where I have learned not to keep things. You avoid accidents such as electrical problems when you use the oven the right way.

EGG ENGLISH MUFFINS

Prep time: 5 minutes | Cook time: 8 minutes | Serves 4

Ingredients

- 4 eggs
- Salt and pepper, to taste
- Olive oil
- 4 English muffins, split
- 1 cup shredded Colby Jack cheese
- 4 slices ham or Canadian bacon

Directions

- Preheat air fryer oven to 390°F (200°C).
- Beat together eggs and add salt and pepper to taste. Spray air fryer cooking tray lightly with oil and add eggs. Bake for 2 minutes, stir, and continue cooking for 3 or 4 minutes, stirring every minute, until eggs are scrambled to your preference. Remove the cooking tray from oven.
- Place bottom halves of English muffins in air fryer cooking tray. Take half of the shredded cheese and divide it among the muffins. Top each with a slice of ham and one-quarter of the eggs. Sprinkle the remaining cheese on top of the eggs. Use a fork to press the cheese into the egg a little so it doesn't slip off before it melts.
- Select Toast, cook at 360°F (180°C) for 1 minute. Add English muffin tops and toast for 2 to 4 minutes to heat through and toast the muffins.

SCOTCH EGGS

Prep time: 10 minutes | Cook time: 15 minutes | Serves 4

Ingredients

- 1 pound (454 g) bulk pork sausage
- 2 tablespoons finely chopped fresh parsley
- 1 tablespoon finely chopped fresh chives
- ⅛ teaspoon freshly grated nutmeg
- ⅛ teaspoon kosher salt
- ⅛ teaspoon black pepper
- 4 hard-cooked large eggs, peeled
- 1 cup shredded Parmesan cheese
- Vegetable oil spray
- Coarse mustard, for serving

Directions

- In a large bowl, gently mix the sausage, parsley, chives, nutmeg, salt, and pepper until well combined. Shape the mixture into four equal-size patties.
- Place one egg on each sausage patty and shape the sausage around the egg, covering it completely. Dredge each sausage-covered egg in the shredded cheese to cover completely, pressing lightly to adhere. (Make sure the cheese well adheres to the meat so shreds of cheese don't end up flying around in the oven.)
- Arrange the Scotch eggs in the air fryer cooking tray. Spray lightly with vegetable oil spray. Select Air Fry. Set temperature to 400°F (205°C), and set time to 15 minutes. Halfway through the cooking time, turn eggs and spray again.
- Serve with mustard.

PEACH BREAD

Prep time: 7 min | Cook time: 35 min | Serves: 4

Ingredients

- Baking soda: 1 tsp.
- Vegetable oil: ⅓ cup
- Cinnamon: 1 tsp.
- Salt: ¼ tsp.
- Flour: 1 ½ cups
- Sugar: half cup
- 3 eggs
- 1 peach, diced with skin
- Baking powder: 1 tsp.
- Glaze
- Milk: 2 tbsp.
- Powdered sugar: ⅓ cup

Directions

- Let the Breville Smart air fryer oven preheat to 350° F with Bake mode.
- In a bowl, add all wet ingredients and sugar.
- In a bowl, add dry ingredients and mix.
- Add the wet ingredients to dry and mix until batter forms.
- Add diced peaches. Oil spray a loaf pan and pour the batter.
- Bake for 35 minutes at 350° F. Cover with foil if tops become brown and not cooked yet.
- In a bowl, add all ingredients of glaze and mix.
- Pour over the bread and serve warm.

CHOCOLATE ALMOND CRESCENT ROLLS

Prep time: 5 minutes | Cook time: 8 minutes | Serves 4 to 6

Directions

- 1 (8-ounce / 227-g) tube of crescent roll dough
- ⅔ cup semi-sweet or bittersweet chocolate chunks
- 1 egg white, lightly beaten
- ¼ cup sliced almonds
- Powder sugar, for dusting
- Butter or oil

Directions

- Preheat the air fryer oven to 350ºF (175ºC).
- Unwrap the crescent roll dough and separate it into triangles with the points facing away from you. Place a row of chocolate chunks along the bottom edge of the dough. (If you are using chips, make it a double row.) Roll the dough up around the chocolate and then place another row of chunks on the dough. Roll again and finish with one or two chocolate chunks. Be sure to leave the end free of chocolate so that it can adhere to the rest of the roll.
- Brush the tops of the crescent rolls with the lightly beaten egg white and sprinkle the almonds on top, pressing them into the crescent dough so they adhere.
- Brush the bottom of the air fryer cooking tray with butter or oil and transfer the crescent rolls to the air fryer cooking tray. Select Air Fry. Set temperature to 350ºF (175ºC), and set time to 8 minutes. Remove and let the crescent rolls cool before dusting with powdered sugar and serve.

PIZZA DOUGH CINNAMON ROLLS

Prep time: 5 min | Cook time: 10 min | Serves: 8

Ingredients

- Cinnamon: 2 tsp.
- Powdered sugar: 2 tsp.
- Brown sugar: ¼ cup
- 1 pizza dough

Directions

- Roll the pizza dough into a rectangle.
- Melt the brown sugar with cinnamon for 20 seconds in the microwave.
- Let the Breville Smart air fryer oven preheat to 400° F with Bake mode.
- Spread the mixture on the pizza dough and roll. Cut them into small pieces, and place them on the air fryer tray.
- Bake in the Breville Smart air fryer oven for seven minutes, till golden brown. Add powdered sugar on top and serve.

CARROT AND RAISIN MUFFINS

Prep time: 10 minutes | Cook time: 12 minutes | Makes 8 muffins

Ingredients

- 1½ cups whole-wheat pastry flour
- 1 teaspoon low-sodium baking powder
- ⅓ cup brown sugar
- ½ teaspoon ground cinnamon
- 1 egg
- 2 egg whites
- ⅔ cup almond milk
- 3 tablespoons safflower oil
- ½ cup finely shredded carrots
- ⅓ cup golden raisins, chopped

Directions

- In a medium bowl, combine the flour, baking powder, brown sugar, and cinnamon, and mix well.
- In a small bowl, combine the egg, egg whites, almond milk, and oil and beat until combined. Stir the egg mixture into the dry ingredients just until combined. Don't overbeat; some lumps should be in the batter—that's just fine.
- Stir the shredded carrot and chopped raisins gently into the batter.
- Double up 16 foil muffin cups to make 8 cups. Put 4 of the cups into the oven and fill ¾ full with the batter.
- Select Bake. Set time to 12 minutes or until the tops of the muffins spring back when lightly touched with your finger.
- Repeat with remaining muffin cups and the remaining batter. Cool the muffins on a wire rack for 10 minutes before serving.

DELICIOUS DONUT HOLES

Prep time: 15 minutes | Cook time: 8 minutes | Makes 12 donut holes

Ingredients

- 1 tablespoon ground flaxseed
- 1½ tablespoons water
- ¼ cup non-dairy milk, unsweetened
- 2 tablespoons neutral-flavored oil (sunflower, safflower, or refined coconut)
- 1½ teaspoons vanilla
- 1½ cups whole-wheat pastry flour or all-purpose gluten-free flour
- ¾ cup coconut sugar, divided
- 2½ teaspoons cinnamon, divided
- ½ teaspoon nutmeg
- ¼ teaspoon sea salt
- ¾ teaspoon baking powder
- Cooking oil spray (refined coconut, sunflower, or safflower)

Directions

- In a medium bowl, stir the flaxseed with the water and set aside for 5 minutes, or until gooey and thick.
- Add the milk, oil, and vanilla. Stir well and set this wet mixture aside.
- In a small bowl, combine the flour, ½ cup coconut sugar, ½ teaspoon cinnamon, nutmeg, salt, and baking powder. Stir very well. Add this mixture to the wet mixture and stir together—it will be stiff, so you'll need to knead it lightly, just until all of the ingredients are thoroughly combined.
- Spray the air fryer cooking tray with oil. Pull off bits of the dough and roll into balls (about 1 inch in size each). Place in the cooking tray, leaving room in between as they'll increase in size a smidge. (You'll need to work in batches, as you probably won't be able to cook all 12 at a time.) Spray the tops with oil and select Air Fry, and set time to 6 minutes.
- Remove the pan, spray the donut holes with oil again, flip them over, and spray them with oil again. Air fry them for 2 minutes, or until golden-brown.
- During these last 2 minutes of frying, place the remaining 4 tablespoons coconut sugar and 2 teaspoons cinnamon in a bowl, and stir to combine.
- When the donut holes are done frying, remove them one at a time and coat them as follows: Spray with oil again and toss

with the cinnamon sugar mixture. Spray one last time, and coat with the cinnamon sugar one last time. Enjoy fresh and warm if possible, as they're the best that way.

OMELET EGG BITES

Prep time: 10 min | Cook time: 13 min | Serves: 12

Ingredients

- 4 eggs
- Diced bell peppers: ¼ cup
- Milk: ½ cup
- Salt: 1 tsp.
- Diced ham: ¼ cup
- Black pepper: ½ tsp.
- Shredded cheese: ¼ cup

Directions

- In a bowl, add eggs and the rest of the ingredients, mix well.
- Oil spray a silicone muffin mold.
- Pour the mixture into the cups.
- Let the air fryer heat to 350° F, place the mold in the air fryer.
- Air fry for 10 minutes, flip and air fry for three minutes more.
- Serve right away.

APPLE SAUCE-WALNUT MUFFINS

Prep time: 15 minutes | Cook time: 20 minutes | Makes 8 muffins

Ingredients

- 1 cup flour
- ⅓ cup sugar
- 1 teaspoon baking powder
- ¼ teaspoon baking soda
- ¼ teaspoon salt
- 1 teaspoon cinnamon
- ¼ teaspoon ginger
- ¼ teaspoon nutmeg
- 1 egg
- 2 tablespoons pancake syrup, plus 2 teaspoons
- 2 tablespoons melted butter, plus 2 teaspoons
- ¾ cup unsweetened applesauce
- ½ teaspoon vanilla extract
- ¼ cup chopped walnuts
- ¼ cup diced apple
- 8 foil muffin cups, liners removed and sprayed with cooking spray

Directions

- Preheat air fryer to 330ºF (165ºC).
- In a large bowl, stir together flour, sugar, baking powder, baking soda, salt, cinnamon, ginger, and nutmeg.
- In a small bowl, beat egg until frothy. Add syrup, butter, applesauce, and vanilla and mix well.
- Pour egg mixture into dry ingredients and stir until just moistened.
- Gently stir in nuts and diced apple.
- Divide batter among the 8 muffin cups.
- Place 4 muffin cups in air fryer cooking tray and select Bake. Set temperature to 330ºF (165ºC), and set time to 9 to 11 minutes.
- Repeat with the remaining 4 muffins or until toothpick inserted in center comes out clean.

EGGS IN A BASKET

Prep time: 5 minutes | Cook time: 6 minutes | Serves 1

Ingredients

- 1 thick slice country, sourdough, or Italian bread
- 2 tablespoons (28 g) unsalted butter, melted
- 1 egg
- Kosher salt and pepper, to taste

Directions

- Brush the bottom of the air fryer cooking tray insert and both sides of the bread with melted butter. Using a small round cookie or biscuit cutter, cut a hole out of the middle of the bread and set it aside.
- Place the slice of bread in the air fryer cooking tray insert. Crack the egg into the hole in the bread, taking care not to break the yolk. Season with salt and pepper. Place the cut-out bread hole next to the slice of bread. Place the cooking tray insert into the oven.
- Select Bake. Set temperature to 300ºF (150ºC), and set time to 6 to 8 minutes until the egg white is set but the yolk is still runny. Using a silicone spatula, remove the bread slice to a plate. Serve with the cut-out bread circle on the side or place it on top of the egg.

Prep time: 15 min | Cook time: 15 min | Serves: 3-4

Ingredients

Dough

- Baking soda: ¼ tsp.
- Vegetable oil: ½ cup
- Buttermilk: ⅓ cup
- Salt: ¼ tsp.
- Flour: 2 cups

Filling

- Sugar: ½ cup
- Nutmeg: ½ tsp.
- Water: ½ cup
- Blackberries: 2 cups
- Corn starch: 1 tbsp.
- Lemon juice: 1 tbsp.
- Cinnamon: ¾ tsp.

Directions

- In a bowl, add flour, salt and baking soda.
- In another bowl, add oil and buttermilk.
- Mix the wet into dry ingredients. Mix with hands until dough forms.
- Roll into ¼ of thickness.
- With a four-inch biscuit cutter, cut all the dough into circles.
- In a pan, add spices, corn starch, lemon juice, sugar and water on medium flame.
- Add blackberries. Keep mixing and let it come to a boil. Turn the heat off and let it cool.
- In each biscuit pie, add 1 tbsp. of blackberry filling and fold in half.
- Seal the edges.
- Preheat the Breville Smart air fryer oven to 350° F.
- Bake for 5 minutes on each side.
- Serve right away with a glaze on top.

Prep time: 10 min | Cook time: 10 min | Serves: 8

Ingredients

- Onion powder: 1 tsp.
- Crescent rolls: 8 oz.
- 6 cooked bacon strips, crumbled

Directions

- Let the Breville Smart air fryer oven preheat to 350° F. Cut the dough into 8 triangles.
- Toss the bacon with onion powder. Save the 1 tbsp. of bacon.
- Add the rest to the triangles and roll. Add 1 tbsp. of bacon on top and press into the dough.
- Air fry for 8 to 10 minutes side down. Serve right away.

BREAKFAST DUMPLINGS

Prep time: 10 min | Cook time: 10 min | Serves: 2

Ingredients

- Swiss cheese: 1 tbsp.
- Wonton wrappers: 8
- Crumbled cooked bacon: 1 tbsp.
- Salt, to taste
- Egg whites: ½ cup

Directions

- In a microwave-safe mug, add egg, salt and cheese. Microwave for 1 ½ minute until cheese melts and eggs are set.
- Add bacon and let it cool for 5 minutes.
  Add this mixture to each of the wrappers. Seal the edges with water.
- In the air fryer tray, place the dumplings and air fry for 5 minutes at 375° F, until crispy and golden.

BACON & EGG BREAKFAST BOMBS

Prep time: 10 min | Cook time: 25 min | Serves: 8

Ingredients

- Black pepper, to taste
- Sharp Cheddar cheese: 10 small cubes
- 4 bacon slices, cut in half-inch pieces
- 5 Buttermilk biscuits, (1 can)
- Butter: 1 tbsp.
- 1 egg mixed with 1 tbsp. water
- 2 eggs, whisked

Directions

- In a skillet, cook bacon until crispy. Take out on a paper towel.
- Add butter into the skillet, melt the butter.
- Whisk eggs with black pepper.
- Pour eggs into the skillet and cook until still moist. Turn off the heat and add bacon. Let it cool for 5 minutes.
- Separate 5 biscuits into two layers.
- In each biscuit, add egg mixture. Add cheese cube on top.
- Fold pinch the edges.
- Brush each biscuit bomb with egg wash.
- Let the Breville Smart air fryer oven preheat to 325° F at Bake.
- Place the bombs in the air fryer tray
- Cook for 8 minutes or more

CHEESE & VEGGIE EGG CUPS

Prep time: 5 min | Cook time: 10 min | Serves: 4

Ingredients

- Minced cilantro: 1 tbsp.
- Cream: 4 tbsp.
- 4 eggs
- Vegetables: 1 cup, diced
- Shredded cheese: 1 cup
- Salt & black pepper, to taste

Directions

- Take 4 ramekins and coat them will oil spray.
- In a bowl, mix eggs with half cheese, cilantro, black pepper, salt, cream, and vegetables.
- Pour the mixture in all ramekins equally.
- Let the Breville Smart air fryer oven preheat to 300° F.
- Place ramekins in the air fryer and air fry for 12 minutes
- Add cheese on top and air fry for 2 minutes more at 400° F.

VEGETABLE EGG SOUFFLÉ

Prep time: 10 min | Cook time: 20 min | Serves: 4

Ingredients

- 4 large eggs
- 1 tsp onion powder
- 1 tsp garlic powder
- 1 tsp red pepper, crushed
- ½ cup broccoli florets, chopped
- ½ cup mushrooms, chopped

Directions

- Sprinkle four ramekins with cooking spray and set aside.
- In a bowl, whisk eggs with onion powder, garlic powder, and red pepper.
- Add mushrooms and broccoli and stir well.
- Pour egg mixture into the prepared ramekins and place ramekins into your air fryer oven.
- Cook at 350° F for 15 minutes. Make sure soufflé is cooked if soufflé is not cooked then cook for 5 minutes more.
- Serve and enjoy.

CRISPY SRIRACHA SPRING ROLLS

Prep time: 50 min | Cook time: 10 min | Serves: 12

Ingredients

- Coleslaw mix: 3 cups
- Cream cheese: 16 oz., softened
- Soy sauce: 1 tbsp.
- Sesame oil: 1 tsp.
- 24 spring roll wrappers
- Chicken breasts: 1 lb., boneless & skinless
- 3 green onions, diced
- Seasoned salt: 1 tsp.
- Sriracha chili sauce: 2 tbsp.

Directions

- Let the Breville Smart air fryer oven preheat to 360° F.
- In a bowl, mix soy sauce, sesame oil, coleslaw mix, and green onions.
- Place chicken on the tray of the air fryer. Cook for 18 to 20 minutes until the internal temperature, reaches 165°.
- Take chicken out, chop and season with salt.
- Change air fryer temperature to 400° F.
- In a bowl, mix cream cheese and sriracha. Add chicken and coleslaw mixture.
- In each wrapper, add some of the fillings. Seal the edges with water and roll tightly.
- Oil spray the rolls and air fry the rolls for 5 to 6 minutes, flip and oil spray, air fry for 5 to 6 minutes.
- Serve with green onions on top

ZUCCHINI FRIES

Prep time: 25 min | Cook time: 12 min | Serves: 4

Ingredients

Garlic Aioli

- Olive oil: 2 tbsp.
- Salt & pepper, to taste
- Mayonnaise: ½ cup
- Roasted garlic: 1 tsp.
- ½ lemon's juice

Zucchini Fries

- 1 large zucchini, sliced into half-inch sticks
- Flour: ½ cup
- Seasoned breadcrumbs: 1 cup
- 2 eggs, whisked
- Salt & Pepper

Directions

- In a bowl, add all ingredients of aioli and mix. Adjust seasoning.
- In a bowl, add flour and season with salt and pepper.
- In another bowl, add whisked eggs.
- In the third bowl, add seasoned breadcrumbs.
- Coat the zucchini fries in flour, then in eggs and lastly in breadcrumbs.
- Place them on the air fryer tray. Let them rest for 10 minutes.
- Let the Breville Smart air fryer oven preheat to 400° F.
- Oil spray the zucchini fries and air fry for 12 minutes, flipping halfway through.
- Serve with aioli.

STUFFED JALAPEÑO

Prep time: 10 min | Cook time: 10 min | Serves: 4

Ingredients

- 1 lb. ground pork sausage
- 1 (8 oz.) package cream cheese, softened
- 1 cup shredded Parmesan cheese
- 1 lb. large fresh jalapeño peppers halved lengthwise and seeded
- 1 (8 oz.) bottle ranch dressing

Directions

- in mix pork sausage ground with ranch dressing and cream cheese in a bowl. But the jalapeño in half and remove their seeds. Divide the cream cheese mixture into the jalapeño halves.
- Place the jalapeño pepper in a baking tray. Set the Baking tray inside the air fryer toaster oven and close the lid. Select the Bake mode at 350° F for 10 minutes. Serve warm.

GARLIC KNOTS

Prep time: 10 min | Cook time: 20 min | Serves: 4-5

Ingredients

- Kosher salt: ¾ tsp.
- 3 minced garlic cloves
- Whole wheat flour: 1 cup
- Greek yogurt: 1 cup
- Butter: 2 tsp.
- Parmesan cheese: 1 tbsp., grated
- Baking powder: 2 tsp.
- Fresh parsley: 1 tbsp., chopped

Directions

- Let the Breville Smart air fryer oven preheat to 375° F.
- In a bowl, add flour, salt and baking powder and mix.
- Add yogurt and make it into a soft dough.
- Divide into 8 pieces and roll each piece into 9" long strip.
- Make each strip into a knotted ball, and place it on the tray.
- Oil spray the buns.
- Let the Breville Smart air fryer oven preheat to 325° F.
- Air fry the knots for 11-12 minutes.
- In a pan, add butter and garlic cook for few minutes.
- Brush the knots with garlic butter and serve.

BACON AVOCADO FRIES

Prep time: 10 min | Cook time: 5 min | Serves: 24

Ingredients

- Ranch dressing: ¼ cup
- 3 avocados
- Bacon: 24 strips

Directions

- Cut every avocado into 8 wedges. Wrap each wedge in the strip of bacon.
- Let the Breville Smart air fryer oven preheat to 400° F.
- Air fry the wedges for 8 minutes.
- Serve with ranch.

MAC & CHEESE BALLS

Prep time: 60 min | Cook time: 12 min | Serves: 16

Ingredients

- Seasoned breadcrumbs: 2 cups
- Leftover mac & cheese: 4 cups
- 2 eggs whisked

Directions

- Keep the leftovers in the fridge for 3 hours.
- Make into 16 balls. Coat the ball in egg then in crumbs.
- Keep in the fridge for half an hour.
- Let the Breville Smart air fryer oven preheat to 360° F.
- Air fry the balls for 10 to 12 minutes. Serve with spicy ketchup.

AIR FRYER RAVIOLI

Prep time: 10 min | Cook time: 10 min | Serves: 17

Ingredients

- Seasoned breadcrumbs: 1 cup
- Optional fresh minced basil
- Cooking spray
- Marinara sauce: 1 cup, warmed.
- Shredded Parmesan cheese: ¼ cup
- Dried basil: 2 tsp.
- All-purpose flour: ½ cup
- Eggs: 2 large, lightly beaten.
- Frozen beef ravioli: 9 oz., thawed.

Directions

- Preheat the fryer to 350° F.
- Mix the breadcrumbs, the Parmesan cheese, and the basil in a bowl. In different bowls, position the flour & eggs.
- To cover all ends, dip the ravioli in flour; shake off the waste. Dip in the eggs, then pat in the crumb mixture to help adhere to the coating.
- Arrange the ravioli in batches in the air fryer in a single layer, dust with cooking spray. Then Cook until crispy brown, 3 to 4 minutes. Flip; spritz with spray for cooking. Cook until crispy brown, 3 to 4 minutes longer. Sprinkle instantly with basil and

extra Parmesan cheese if needed. With marinara sauce, serve warm.

ONION RINGS

Prep time: 10 min | Cook time: 10 min | Serves: 4

Ingredients

- Mayo: ⅓ cup
- Ketchup: 1 ½ -2 tbsp.
- Creamy horseradish: 1-2 tbsp.
- Smoked paprika: ½ tsp.
- Oregano: ½ tsp.
- Salt & Pepper
- Vidalia onion: 1 large (peeled). Mine weighed 12oz.
- Panko breadcrumbs: 1 ½ cup
- Buttermilk: 1 cup
- Beaten: 1 egg.
- Flour: 1 cup
- Smoked paprika: 1 tsp.
- Garlic powder: 1 tsp.
- Optional Dipping Sauce

Directions

- Spray the air fryer with cooking oil.
- Cut stems off all onion sides. Cut onion into rounds that are ½" thick. There are wobbly onions. When chopping, be patient and if necessary, use a mandolin. Before you slice, attempt to stabilize the onion.
- In a large bowl, add the flour. With the garlic powder, smoked paprika, salt, & pepper to taste, season the flour.
- To seasoned flour, add the egg and buttermilk. Beat & stir to blend together.
- In a separate bowl, add the panko breadcrumbs.
- Dredge the sliced onions and the panko breadcrumbs in the flour buttermilk blend.

- On a tray, put the onion rings. For 15 minutes, Freeze the onion rings after onions breading.
- In an air fryer, put the onions. Don't leave them stacked. If required, cook in batches.
- With cooking oil, spray it.
- Cook at 370° F for 10-12 minutes. To determine that both sides are crisp and golden brown, check in on yours. If required, flip.

BACON-WRAPPED CHICKEN BITES

Prep time: 10 min | Cook time: 8 min | Serves: 10

Ingredients

- Skinless, boneless chicken breast 1.25 lbs. 3, cut in 1" chunks (30 pieces)
- Optional, for dipping duck sauce/Thai sweet chili sauce
- Centre cut bacon 10 slices, cut into thirds.

Directions

- Preheat the fryer.
- Wrap a bacon piece around each chicken piece and secure it with a toothpick.
- For 8 minutes in batches, air fry in an even 400° F layer, rotating halfway till chicken is cooked and browned is the bacon.
- Blot it on a paper towel & serve it immediately.

NASHVILLE CAULIFLOWER BITES

Prep time: 35 min | Cook time: 20 min | Serves: 4

Ingredients

Spice Mix

- Cayenne: 2 tsp.
- Paprika: 1 tbsp.
- Garlic powder: 2 tsp.
- Mustard powder: 2 tsp.
- Onion powder: 2 tsp.
- Freshly ground black pepper: 2 tsp.

Cauliflower

- Cauliflower florets: 1 lb.
- Salt, to taste

Batter

- Hot sauce: 1 tbsp.
- Buttermilk: 1 cup
- Dry breadcrumbs: 1 cup
- Flour: ½ cup

Directions

- Add all spices to a bowl and mix.
- Add cauliflower in a different bowl and toss with salt. Add to the spice bowl and toss. Marinate in the fridge for 30 minutes, covered.
- Let your air fryer preheat to 350° F.
- In a dish, add the batter ingredients and mix. In a separate bowl, add the breadcrumbs.
- Coat the vegetable in the batter, and then in breadcrumbs. Oil spray the basket.
- Cook in air fry for 15 minutes and serve.

MOZZARELLA STICKS

Prep time: 40 min | Cook time: 20min | Serves: 4

Ingredients

- 1 Egg beaten
- 2 tbsp. Milk
- 4 Mozzarella cheese sticks cut in half
- 1 tsp. Italian seasoning
- ½ tsp. Salt
- 1 cup Panko breadcrumbs

Directions

- Cut the mozzarella sticks in half and place them in the freezer for at least 30 minutes.
- 3 bowls are required. In one bowl, whisk together the egg and milk; in another, combine everything else.
- Preheat your air fryer to 400° F. Dip the stick in the egg mixture first, then the panko crumbs, then back in the egg and crumbs until fully coated. Place the dish on the rack.
- Continue until all of the other sticks have been completed.
- Return for another 8 minutes, flipping halfway through. When they turn brownish, keep an eye on them and remove them.
- Toss with marinara sauce and serve.

RADISH CHIPS

Prep time: 10 min | Cook time: 20 min | Serves: 4

Ingredients

- Radishes, leaves removed and cleaned
- Salt to season
- Water
- Cooking spray

Directions

- Using a mandolin, slice the radishes thinly. Put them in a pot and pour water on them. Heat the pot on a stovetop, and bring to boil, until the radishes are translucent, for 4 minutes. After 4 minutes, drain the radishes through a sieve; set aside. Grease the fryer basket with cooking spray.
- Add in the radish slices and cook for 8 minutes, flipping once halfway through. Cook until golden brown, at 400° F. Meanwhile, prepare a paper towel-lined plate. Once the radishes are ready, transfer them to the paper towel-lined plate. Season with salt, and serve with ketchup or garlic mayo.

BREADED MUSHROOMS

Prep time: 10 min | Cook time: 45 min | Serves: 4

Ingredients

- 1 lb. small Button mushrooms, cleaned
- 1 cups breadcrumbs
- 2 eggs, beaten
- Salt and pepper to taste
- 2 cups Parmigiano Reggiano cheese, grated

Directions

- Preheat the air fryer to 360° F. Pour the breadcrumbs in a bowl, add salt and pepper and mix well. Pour the cheese in a separate bowl and set aside. Dip each mushroom in the eggs, then in the crumbs, and then in the cheese.
- Slide out the fryer basket and add 6 to 10 mushrooms. Cook them for 20 minutes, in batches, if needed. Serve with cheese dip.

ASIAN FIVE-SPICE CHICKEN WINGS

Prep time: 5 minutes | Cook time: 13 minutes | Serves 4

Ingredients

- 2 pounds (907 g) chicken wings
- ½ cup Asian-style salad dressing
- 2 tablespoons Chinese five-spice powder

Directions

- Cut off wing tips and discard or freeze for stock. Cut remaining wing pieces in two at the joint.
- Place wing pieces in a large sealable plastic bag. Pour in the Asian dressing, seal bag, and massage the marinade into the wings until well coated. Refrigerate for at least an hour.
- Remove wings from bag, drain off excess marinade, and place wings in air fryer cooking tray.
- Select Air Fry. Set temperature to 360°F (180°C), and set time to 13 to 15 minutes or until juices run clear. About halfway through cooking time, shake the cooking tray or stir wings for more even cooking.
- Transfer cooked wings to plate in a single layer. Sprinkle half of the Chinese five-spice powder on the wings, turn, and sprinkle other side with remaining seasoning.

VEGAN AVOCADO FRIES

Prep time: 10 minutes | Cook time: 10 minutes | Serves 4

Ingredients

- ¼ cup almond or coconut milk
- 1 tablespoon lime juice
- ⅛ teaspoon hot sauce
- 2 tablespoons flour
- ¾ cup panko breadcrumbs
- ¼ cup cornmeal
- ¼ teaspoon salt
- 1 large avocado
- Oil for misting or cooking spray

Directions

- In a small bowl, whisk together the almond or coconut milk, lime juice, and hot sauce.
- Place flour on a sheet of wax paper.
- Mix panko, cornmeal, and salt and place on another sheet of wax paper.
- Split avocado in half and remove pit. Peel or use a spoon to lift avocado halves out of the skin.
- Cut avocado lengthwise into ½-inch slices. Dip each in flour, then milk mixture, then roll in panko mixture.
- Mist with oil or cooking spray and select Roast. Set temperature to 390°F (200°C), and set time to 10 minutes, until the crust is brown and crispy.

AIR FRIED PITA CHIPS

Prep time: 5 minutes | Cook time: 6 minutes | Serves 4

Ingredients

- 2 pieces whole-wheat pita bread
- 3 tablespoons olive oil
- 1 teaspoon freshly squeezed lemon juice
- 1 teaspoon salt
- 1 teaspoon dried basil
- 1 teaspoon garlic powder

Directions

- Spray the air fryer cooking tray with olive oil.
- Using a pair of kitchen shears or a pizza cutter, cut the pita bread into small wedges.
- Place the wedges in a small mixing bowl and add the olive oil, lemon juice, salt, dried basil, and garlic powder.
- Mix well, coating each wedge.
- Place the seasoned pita wedges in the greased air fryer cooking tray in a single layer, being careful not to overcrowd them. (You may have to bake the pita chips in more than one batch.)
- Select Air Fry. Set temperature to 350°F (180°C), and set time to 6 minutes. Every 2 minutes or so, remove the drawer and shake the pita chips so they redistribute in the cooking tray for even cooking.
- Serve with your choice of dip or alone as a tasty snack.

RED BEETS CHIPS

Prep time: 5 minutes | Cook time: 30 minutes | Serves 4

Ingredients

- 1 pound (454 g) red beets, peeled and cut into ⅛-inch slices
- 1 tablespoon olive oil
- 1 teaspoon cayenne pepper
- Sea salt and ground black pepper, to taste

Directions

- Preheat your Air Fryer oven to 330°F (166°C).
- Toss the beets with the remaining ingredients and place them in the Air Fryer cooking tray.
- Select Air Fry, cook for 30 minutes at 330°F (166°C), shaking the cooking tray occasionally and working in batches.
- Enjoy!

COCONUT SHRIMP

Prep time: 10 min | Cook time: 5 min | Serves: 2

Ingredients

- ½ lb. shrimp
- 1 egg whisked
- ½ cup All-Purpose flour
- ½ cup shredded coconut, unsweetened
- ¼ cup Panko breadcrumbs
- 1 tsp. Cajun seasoning
- 1 tsp. salt
- ¼ tsp. black pepper

Directions

- Preheat the air fryer to 390° F on Air Fry mode.
- Leave the tails on the shrimp and peel them.
- 3 bowls are required. In one dish, combine the flour with all of the seasonings; in another, combine the egg; and in the third, combine the coconut and breadcrumbs.
- Every shrimp should be dipped in flour, then egg, and finally coconut mixture, ensuring that all sides of the shrimp are coated.
- Arrange the shrimp on the rack in a single layer.
- Cook for 3 minutes after gently spraying the shrimp with oil in the middle position.
- Cook for another minute or two after flipping the shrimp after 3 minutes. The shrimp's size will determine the length of time.
- Serve with the sauce
- Serve right away.

AIR FRYER TILAPIA FILLETS

Prep time: 15 min | Cook time: 10 min | Serves: 2

Ingredients

- Black pepper: ½ tsp.
- 2 tilapia filets
- Olive oil: 1 tbsp.
- Ground thyme: ½ tsp.
- Smoked paprika: 1 ½ tbsp.
- Garlic powder: ¼ tsp.
- Dried oregano: ½ tsp.
- Onion powder: 1 ½ tsp.
- Cayenne pepper: ½ tsp.
- Sea salt: ½ tsp.
- Lemon wedges

Directions

- In a bowl, add all spices and mix.
- Coat the fish with oil and sprinkle spice mix on top, and coat the fish. let it rest for 15 minutes.
- Let the Breville Smart air fryer oven preheat to 350° F.
- Put the fish on the air fryer tray. Air fry for 6 minutes.
- Flip and air fry for 4-6 minutes. (or do not flip).
- Serve with lemon wedges.

Prep time: 15 min | Cook time: 10 min | Serves: 2

Ingredients

- 1 scallion, diced
- 1 egg, whisked
- Lump crab meat: ½ lb.
- Milk: 1 tbsp.
- Panko breadcrumbs: ½ cup
- Old bay seasoning: ¼ tsp.
- Dijon mustard: 1 tsp.
- Hot sauce, a dash
- Diced red bell pepper: ¼ cup
- Lemon juice: 1 ½ tsp.
- Worcestershire sauce: ½ tsp.
- Salt & black pepper, to taste

Directions

- In a bowl, whisk the eggs with milk. Add breadcrumbs (¼ cup).
- In a bowl, add the rest of the ingredients except for crab meat and breadcrumbs.
- Mix and add crab meat; add breadcrumb mixture. Make into 4 patties.
- Let the Breville Smart air fryer oven preheat to 375° F.
- On a plate, add the rest of the breadcrumbs. Coat the patties in breadcrumbs.
- Spray the patties with oil and place them on the air fryer tray.
- Air fry for 5 minutes, flip and cook for 5 more minutes.
- Serve with tartar sauce.

Prep time: 15 min | Cook time: 25 min | Serves: 2

Ingredients

- 1 potato
- Grated Parmesan cheese: 1 ½ tsp.
- Olive oil: 1 tbsp.
- All-purpose flour: 3 tbsp.
- Haddock fillets: ½ lb.
- 1 egg
- Water: 2 tbsp.
- Cayenne pepper, a pinch
- Salt & pepper: to taste
- Crushed cornflakes: ⅓ cup

Directions

- Let the Breville Smart air fryer oven preheat to 400° F.
- Cut the potato into half-inch sticks.
- Toss the potatoes with oil, salt and pepper.
- Spread the chips on the air fry tray and air fry for 5 to 10 minutes, until crispy and light brown.
- In a bowl, add black pepper and flour. In another bowl, whisk the egg with water.
- In another bowl, add cheese, cayenne and cornflakes.
- Season the fish with salt, coat the fish in flour, then egg, and finally in cornflakes mixture.
- Place the fish on the tray and air fry for 8 to 10 minutes.
- Serve with chips.
- fryer.
- Air fry for 10 minutes, serve right away.

HONEY SRIRACHA SALMON

Prep time: 25 min | Cook time: 7 min | Serves: 2

Ingredients

- Honey: 3 tbsp.
- Salmon: 1 ½ lbs.
- Salt, to taste
- Sriracha: 2 tbsp.

Directions

- In a bowl, mix honey and sriracha.
- Season the fish with salt and pour the sriracha mixture on the fish.
- Let it rest for 20 minutes.
- Let the Breville Smart air fryer oven preheat to 400° F.
- Place the fish on the air fryer tray and air fry for 7 minutes.
- Serve right away.

FISH STICKS

Prep time: 10 min | Cook time: 30 min | Serves: 2

Ingredients

- Cod: 1 ½ lbs.
- Onion powder: 1 ½ tsp.
- 2 eggs
- Almond flour: 1 cup
- Tapioca starch: ½ cup
- Dried dill: 1 ½ tsp.
- Sea salt: 1 tsp.
- Black pepper: 1 tsp.
- Mustard powder: ½ tsp.

For tartar sauce

- Dill relish: 1 tbsp.
- Salt: ¼ tsp.
- Dried herbs: 1 tbsp.
- Avocado oil mayo: ⅓ cup
- Lemon juice: 2 tsp.

Directions

- Let the Breville Smart air fryer oven preheat to 390° F.
- Season the fish with salt and pepper.
- Slice the fish into sticks (half an inch by half an inch)
- In a bowl, add starch. In another bowl, whisk the eggs.
- In a bowl, whisk onion powder, almond flour, mustard powder, dill, salt and pepper.
- Coat the fish in starch, then in eggs and lastly in a flour mixture.
- Oil spray the air fry tray generously and place the fish sticks on it.
- Spray the fish sticks with oil.
- Air fry for 11 minutes, flipping halfway through.
- In a bowl, add all the ingredients of tartar sauce, mix and serve with fish sticks.

LOBSTER TAILS WITH LEMON-GARLIC BUTTER

Prep time: 10 min | Cook time: 10 min | Serves: 2

Ingredients

- 2 lobster tails
- 4 tbsp. butter
- 1 tsp. lemon zest
- 1 clove garlic, grated
- Salt & pepper to taste
- 1 tsp. chopped fresh parsley

Directions

- Butter lobster tails use kitchen shears to cut lengthwise through the hard top shells and meat centres. Cut to the bottoms of the eggs, but not into them. Separate the tail halves. With the lobster meat facing up, place the tails in the air fryer basket.
- In a small saucepan over medium heat, melt the butter. Heat the lemon zest and garlic for around 30 seconds or until the garlic is tender. Brush 2 tbsp. of the butter mixture onto lobster tails in a small bowl; discard any remaining brushed butter to prevent contamination from raw lobster. Season the lobster with salt and pepper before eating.
- Cook for 5 to 7 minutes in an air fryer at 380° F until lobster meat is opaque. Place the lobster meat on a plate with the reserved butter from the saucepan. Serve with lemon wedges and parsley on top.

POPCORN SHRIMP TACOS

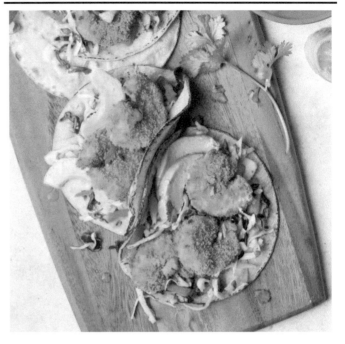

Prep time: 10 min | Cook time: 20 min | Serves: 4

Ingredients

- Coleslaw mix: 2 cups
- Lime juice: 2 tbsp.
- Salt: ¼ tsp.
- Minced fresh cilantro: ¼ cup
- Panko breadcrumbs: 1 ½ cups
- 1 jalapeño pepper, chopped without seeds
- Honey: 2 tbsp.
- Uncooked small shrimp: 1 lb., peeled & deveined
- 2 eggs
- Milk: 2 tbsp.
- All-purpose flour: ½ cup
- 8 corn tortillas small
- Ground cumin: 1 tbsp.
- Garlic powder: 1 tbsp.
- Avocado slices

Directions

- In a bowl, add jalapeño, coleslaw mix, honey, salt, cilantro, and lime juice. Toss and set it aside.
- Let the Breville Smart air fryer oven preheat to 375° F.
- In a bowl, whisk eggs with milk. In another bowl, add flour. Add garlic powder, panko, and cumin to another bowl and mix.
- Coat shrimps in flour, then in egg and lastly in panko. Oil spray the shrimps.
- Air fry the shrimps for 2 to 3 minutes on each side.
- In a tortilla, add shrimps, avocado slices and coleslaw mix.

CAJUN CRAB LEGS

Prep time: 5 min | Cook time: 5 min | Serves: 2

Ingredients

- 1 cluster Snow Crab legs
- 2 tbsp. olive oil
- 1 tbsp. Cajun seasoning

Directions

- In a big mixing bowl, add all ingredients and toss well.
- Let the Breville Smart air fryer oven preheat to 350° F.
- Transfer to an air fryer tray and cook for 3 to 5 minutes.
- Serve right away.

BANG BANG SHRIMP

Prep time: 15 min | Cook time: 15 min | Serves: 2

Ingredients

For shrimp

- Buttermilk: 1 cup
- Corn starch with salt & pepper: 1 cup
- 1 egg + 1 tsp. Water
- Shrimp: 2 lbs., peeled & deveined

For the sauce

- Sour cream: ¼ cup
- Sriracha: 1 tbsp.
- Mayonnaise: ¼ cup
- Dill weed, a pinch
- Thai chile sweet sauce: ⅓ cup
- Buttermilk: 2 tbsp.

Directions

- In a bowl, add corn starch.
- In a bowl, add shrimps and buttermilk, toss to coat.
- Coat the shrimps in corn starch and place them on the air fryer tray.
- Brush the shrimps with egg wash and oil spray the shrimps
- Let the Breville Smart air fryer oven preheat to 450° F.
- Air fry for 5 minutes. Flip them.
- Oil spray again, egg wash, air fry for 4-5 minutes.
- In a bowl, add all ingredients of the sauce and mix well.
- Serve with shrimps.

ROSEMARY GARLIC GRILLED PRAWNS

Prep time: 75 min | Cook time: 10 min | Serves: 2

Ingredients

- 8 prawns
- Melted butter: ½ tbsp.
- Rosemary leaves
- Kosher salt & black pepper
- Green capsicum: slices
- 3-4 cloves of minced garlic

Directions

- In a bowl, mix all the ingredients and marinate the prawns in it for at least 60 minutes or more
- Add 2 prawns and 2 slices of capsicum on each skewer.
- Let the Breville Smart air fryer oven preheat to 356° F.
- Air fry the skewers for 5 to 6 minutes. Then change the temperature to 390° F and cook for 1 minute.
- Serve with lemon wedges.

THYME SCALLOPS

Prep time: 5 min | Cook time: 10 min | Serves: 4

Ingredients

- 1 lb. scallops
- Salt and pepper
- ½ tbsp. butter
- ½ cup thyme, chopped

Directions

- Wash the scallops and dry them completely. Season with pepper and salt, then set aside while you prepare the pan.
- Grease a foil pan in several spots with the butter and cover the bottom with the thyme. Place the scallops on top.
- Pre-heat the fryer at 400° F and set the rack inside.
- Place the foil pan on the rack and allow to cook for 7 minutes.
- Take care when removing the pan from the fryer and transfer the scallops to a serving dish. Spoon any remaining butter in the pan over the fish and enjoy.

TASTY GRILLED RED MULLET

Prep time: 5 min | Cook time: 10 min | Serves: 8

Ingredients

- 8 whole red mullets, gutted and scales removed
- Salt and pepper to taste
- Juice from 1 lemon
- 1 tbsp. olive oil

Directions

- Preheat the air fryer at 390° F.
- Place the grill pan attachment in the air fryer.
- Season the red mullet with salt, pepper, and lemon juice.
- Brush with olive oil.
- Grill for 15 minutes.

SALMON WITH PISTACHIO BARK

Prep time: 10 min | Cook time: 30 min | Serves: 4

Ingredients

- 600g salmon fillet
- 50g pistachios
- Salt to taste

Direction:

- Put the parchment paper on the bottom of the air fryer basket and place the salmon fillet in it (it can be cooked whole or already divided into 4 portions).
- Cut the pistachios in thick pieces; grease the top of the fish, salt (just a little because the pistachios are already salted) and cover everything with the pistachios.
- Set the air fryer to 350° F and simmer for 25 minutes.

Air Fryer Shrimp a La Bang

Prep time: 10 min | Cook time: 12 min | Serves: 2

Ingredients

- ½ cup mayonnaise
- ¼ cup sweet chili sauce
- 1 tbsp. sriracha sauce
- ¼ cup all-purpose flour
- 1 cup panko breadcrumbs
- Raw shrimp: 1 lb., peeled and deveined
- 1 leaf lettuce
- 2 green, chopped onions or to taste (optional)

Directions

- Set temperature of air fryer to 400° F.
- In a bowl, stir in mayonnaise, chili sauce, and sriracha sauce until smooth. Put some bang sauce, if desired, in a separate bowl for dipping.

- Take a plate and place flour on it. Use a separate plate and place panko breadcrumbs on it.
- First coat the shrimp with flour, then mayonnaise mixture, then panko. Place shrimp covered on a baking sheet.
- Place shrimp, without overcrowding, in the air fryer basket.
- Cook for approximately 12 minutes. Repeat with shrimp leftover.
- Use lettuce wraps for serving, garnished with green onion.

RESTAURANT-STYLE FRIED CALAMARI RINGS

Prep time: 10 minutes | Cook time: 5 minutes | Serves 4

Ingredients

- 1 cup all-purpose flour
- ½ cup tortilla chips, crushed
- 1 teaspoon mustard powder
- 1 tablespoon dried parsley
- Sea salt and freshly ground black pepper, to taste
- 1 teaspoon cayenne pepper
- 2 tablespoons olive oil
- 1 pound (454 g) calamari, sliced into rings

Directions

- In a mixing bowl, thoroughly combine the flour, tortilla chips, spices, and olive oil. Mix to combine well.
- Now, dip your calamari into the flour mixture to coat.
- Select Air Fry. Set temperature to 400°F (205ºC), and set time to 5 minutes, turning them over halfway through the cooking time.
- Bon appétit!

CAJUN FRIED SHRIMP WITH REMOULADE

Prep time: 20 minutes | Cook time: 8 minutes | Serves 4

Ingredients

For the Remoulade:

- ½ cup mayonnaise
- 1 green onion, finely chopped
- 1 clove garlic, minced
- 1 tablespoon sweet pickle relish
- 2 tablespoons Creole mustard
- 2 teaspoons fresh lemon juice
- ½ teaspoon hot pepper sauce
- ½ teaspoon Worcestershire sauce
- ¼ teaspoon smoked paprika
- ¼ teaspoon kosher salt

For the Shrimp:

- 1½ cups buttermilk
- 1 large egg
- 3 teaspoons salt-free Cajun seasoning
- 1 pound (454 g) jumbo raw shrimp, peeled and deveined
- 2 cups finely ground cornmeal
- Kosher salt and black pepper
- Vegetable oil spray

Directions

Make the Remoulade

- In a small bowl, stir together all the ingredients until well combined. Cover the sauce and chill until serving time.

Make the Shrimp

- In a large bowl, whisk together the buttermilk, egg, and 1 teaspoon of the Cajun seasoning. Add the shrimp and toss gently to combine. Refrigerate for at least 15 minutes, or up to 1 hour.
- Meanwhile, in a shallow dish, whisk together the remaining 2 teaspoons of Cajun seasoning, cornmeal, and salt and pepper to taste.
- Spray the air fryer cooking tray with the vegetable oil spray. Dredge the shrimp in the cornmeal mixture until well coated. Shake off any excess and arrange the shrimp in the air fryer cooking tray. Spray with oil spray.
- Select Air Fry. Set temperature to 350ºF (175ºC), and set time to 8 minutes, carefully turning and spraying the shrimp with the oil spray halfway through the cooking time.
- Serve the shrimp with the remoulade.

TIGER PRAWNS WITH SHERRY WINE

Prep time: 10 minutes | Cook time: 9 minutes | Serves 4

Ingredients

- 1½ pounds (680 g) tiger prawns, peeled and deveined
- 1 tablespoon coconut oil
- 1 teaspoon garlic, crushed
- 1 teaspoon Old Bay seasoning
- Coarse sea salt and ground black pepper, to taste
- ¼ cup sherry wine
- 1 teaspoon Dijon mustard

Directions

- Toss all ingredients in a lightly greased Air Fryer cooking tray.
- Select Air Fry. Set temperature to 400ºF (205ºC), and set time to 9 minutes, tossing the cooking tray halfway through the cooking time.
- Bon appétit!

BUTTERMILK-FRIED DRUMSTICKS

Prep time: 10 minutes | Cook time: 20 minutes | Serves 2

Ingredients

- 1 egg
- ½ cup buttermilk
- ¾ cup self-rising flour
- ¾ cup seasoned panko breadcrumbs
- 1 teaspoon salt
- ¼ teaspoon ground black pepper (to mix into coating)
- 4 chicken drumsticks, skin on
- Oil for misting or cooking spray

Directions

- Beat together egg and buttermilk in shallow dish.
- In a second shallow dish, combine the flour, panko crumbs, salt, and pepper.
- Sprinkle chicken legs with additional salt and pepper to taste.
- Dip legs in buttermilk mixture, then roll in panko mixture, pressing in crumbs to make coating stick. Mist with oil or cooking spray.
- Spray air fryer cooking tray with cooking spray.
- Roast drumsticks at 360°F (180°C), and set time to 10 minutes. Turn pieces over and roast for an additional 10 minutes.
- Turn pieces to check for browning. If you have any white spots that haven't begun to brown, spritz them with oil or cooking spray. Continue cooking for 5 minutes or until crust is golden brown and juices run clear. Larger, meatier drumsticks will take longer to cook than small ones.

SPICED CHICKEN CHIMICHANGAS

Prep time: 15 minutes | Cook time: 10 minutes | Serves 4

Ingredients

- 2 cups cooked chicken, shredded
- 2 tablespoons chopped green chiles
- ½ teaspoon oregano
- ½ teaspoon cumin
- ½ teaspoon onion powder
- ¼ teaspoon garlic powder
- Salt and pepper, to taste
- 8 (6- or 7-inch diameter) flour tortillas
- Oil for misting or cooking spray
- For the Chimichanga Sauce:
- 2 tablespoons butter
- 2 tablespoons flour
- 1 cup chicken broth
- ¼ cup light sour cream
- ¼ teaspoon salt
- 2 ounces (57 g) Pepper Jack or Monterey Jack cheese, shredded

Directions

- Make the sauce by melting butter in a saucepan over medium-low heat. Stir in flour until smooth and slightly bubbly. Gradually add broth, stirring constantly until smooth. Cook and stir for 1 minute, until the mixture slightly thickens. Remove from heat and stir in sour cream and salt. Set aside.
- In a medium bowl, mix together the chicken, chiles, oregano, cumin, onion powder, garlic, salt, and pepper. Stir in 3 to 4 tablespoons of the sauce, using just enough to make the filling moist but not soupy.
- Divide filling among the 8 tortillas. Place filling down the center of tortilla, stopping about 1 inch from edges. Fold one side of tortilla over filling, fold the two sides in, and then roll up. Mist all sides with oil or cooking spray.
- Place chimichangas in air fryer cooking tray seam side down. To fit more into the cooking tray, you can stand them on their sides with the seams against the sides of the cooking tray.

- Select Roast. Set temperature to 360ºF (180ºC), and set time to 8 to 10 minutes or until heated through and crispy brown outside.
- Add the shredded cheese to the remaining sauce. Stir over low heat, warming just until the cheese melts. Don't boil or sour cream may curdle.
- Drizzle the sauce over the chimichangas.

CHICKEN CORDON BLEU

Prep time: 10 minutes | Cook time: 16 minutes | Serves 4

Ingredients

- 4 small boneless, skinless chicken breasts
- Salt and pepper, to taste
- 4 slices deli ham
- 4 (3- to 4-inch square) slices deli Swiss cheese
- 2 tablespoons olive oil
- 2 teaspoons marjoram
- ¼ teaspoon paprika

Directions

- Split each chicken breast horizontally almost in two, leaving one edge intact.
- Lay breasts open flat and sprinkle with salt and pepper to taste.
- Place a ham slice on top of each chicken breast.
- Cut cheese slices in half and place one half atop each breast. Set aside the remaining halves of cheese slices.
- Roll up chicken breasts to enclose cheese and ham and secure with toothpicks.
- Mix together the olive oil, marjoram, and paprika. Rub all over outsides of chicken breasts.
- Place chicken in air fryer cooking tray and select Roast. Set temperature to 360ºF (180ºC), and set time to 15 to 20 minutes, until well done and juices run clear.
- Remove all toothpicks. To avoid burns, place chicken breasts on a plate to remove toothpicks, then immediately return them to the air fryer cooking tray.
- Place a half cheese slice on top of each chicken breast and cook for a minute or so just to melt cheese.

PANKO-CRUSTED CHICKEN NUGGETS

Prep time: 10 minutes | Cook time: 26 minutes | Makes 20 to 24 nuggets

Ingredients

- 1 pound (454 g) boneless, skinless chicken thighs, cut into 1-inch chunks
- ¾ teaspoon salt
- ½ teaspoon black pepper
- ½ teaspoon garlic powder
- ½ teaspoon onion powder
- ½ cup flour
- 2 eggs, beaten
- ½ cup panko breadcrumbs
- 3 tablespoons plain breadcrumbs
- Oil for misting or cooking spray

Directions

- In the bowl of a food processor, combine chicken, ½ teaspoon salt, pepper, garlic powder, and onion powder. Process in short pulses until chicken is very finely chopped and well blended.
- Place flour in one shallow dish and beaten eggs in another. In a third dish or plastic bag, mix together the panko crumbs, plain breadcrumbs, and ¼ teaspoon salt.
- Shape chicken mixture into small nuggets. Dip nuggets in flour, then eggs, then panko crumb mixture.
- Spray nuggets on both sides with oil or cooking spray and place in air fryer cooking tray in a single layer, close but not overlapping.
- Select Air Fry. Set temperature to 360ºF (180ºC), and set time to 10 minutes. Spray with oil and cook 3 to 4 minutes, until chicken is done and coating is golden brown.
- Repeat step 5 to cook the remaining nuggets.

HONEY-LIME GLAZED CORNISH HENS

Prep time: 5 minutes | Cook time: 25 minutes | Serves 2 to 3

Ingredients

- 1 (1½- to 2-pound / 680- to 907-g) Cornish game hen
- 1 tablespoon honey
- 1 tablespoon lime juice
- 1 teaspoon poultry seasoning
- Salt and pepper, to taste
- Cooking spray

Directions

- To split the hen into halves, cut through breast bone and down one side of the backbone.
- Mix the honey, lime juice, and poultry seasoning together and brush or rub onto all sides of the hen. Season to taste with salt and pepper.
- Spray air fryer cooking tray with cooking spray and place hen halves in the cooking tray, skin-side down.
- Select Roast. Set temperature to 330°F (165°C), and set time to 25 to 30 minutes. Hen will be done when juices run clear and can be pierced at leg joint with a fork. Let hen rest for 5 to 10 minutes.

PEANUT BUTTER-BARBECUE CHICKEN

Prep time: 10 minutes | Cook time: 20 minutes | Serves 4

Ingredients

- 1 pound (454 g) boneless, skinless chicken thighs
- Salt and pepper, to taste
- 1 large orange
- ½ cup barbecue sauce
- 2 tablespoons smooth peanut butter
- 2 tablespoons chopped peanuts for garnish (optional)
- Cooking spray

Directions

- Season chicken with salt and pepper to taste. Place in a shallow dish or plastic bag.
- Grate orange peel, squeeze orange and reserve 1 tablespoon of juice for the sauce.
- Pour remaining juice over chicken and marinate for 30 minutes.
- Mix together the reserved 1 tablespoon of orange juice, barbeque sauce, peanut butter, and 1 teaspoon grated orange peel.
- Place ¼ cup of sauce mixture in a small bowl for basting. Set remaining sauce aside to serve with cooked chicken.
- Preheat the oven to 360°F (180°C). Spray cooking tray with nonstick cooking spray.
- Remove chicken from marinade, letting excess drip off. Place in air fryer cooking tray and cook for 5 minutes. Turn chicken over and cook for 5 minutes longer.
- Brush both sides of chicken lightly with sauce.
- Roast chicken 5 minutes, then turn thighs one more time, again brushing both sides lightly with sauce. Roast for 5 more minutes or until chicken is done and juices run clear.
- Serve chicken with remaining sauce on the side and garnish with chopped peanuts if you like.

TURKEY BURGERS

Prep time: 10 minutes | Cook time: 10 minutes | Serves 4

Ingredients

- 1 pound (454 g) ground turkey
- ¼ cup diced red onion
- 1 tablespoon grilled chicken seasoning
- ½ teaspoon dried parsley
- ½ teaspoon salt
- 4 slices provolone cheese
- 4 whole-grain sandwich buns
- Suggested toppings: lettuce, sliced tomatoes, dill pickles, and mustard

Directions

- Combine the turkey, onion, chicken seasoning, parsley, and salt and mix well.
- Shape into 4 patties.
- Select Roast. Set temperature to 360°F (180°C), and set time to 9 to 11 minutes or until turkey is well done and juices run clear.
- Top each burger with a slice of cheese and cook 1 to 2 minutes to melt.
- Serve on buns with your favorite toppings.

SOUTHERN FRIED CHICKEN

Prep time: 10 minutes | Cook time: 26 minutes | Serves 4

Ingredients

- ½ cup buttermilk
- 2 teaspoons salt, plus 1 tablespoon
- 1 teaspoon freshly ground black pepper
- 1 pound (454 g) chicken thighs and drumsticks
- 1 cup all-purpose flour
- 2 teaspoons onion powder
- 2 teaspoons garlic powder
- ½ teaspoon sweet paprika
- cooking spray

Directions

- In a large mixing bowl, whisk together the buttermilk, 2 teaspoons of salt, and pepper.
- Add the chicken pieces to the bowl, and let the chicken marinate for at least an hour, covered, in the refrigerator.
- About 5 minutes before the chicken is done marinating, prepare the dredging mixture. In a large mixing bowl, combine the flour, 1 tablespoon of salt, onion powder, garlic powder, and paprika.
- Spray the air fryer cooking tray with olive oil.
- Remove the chicken from the buttermilk mixture and dredge it in the flour mixture. Shake off any excess flour.
- Place the chicken pieces into the greased air fryer cooking tray in a single layer, leaving space between each piece. (You may have to fry the chicken in more than one batch.) Spray the chicken generously with olive oil.
- Select Air Fry. Set temperature to 390°F (200°C). Set the timer and cook for 13 minutes.
- Using tongs, flip the chicken. Spray generously with olive oil.
- Reset the timer and fry for 13 minutes or more.
- Check that the chicken has reached an internal temperature of 165°F (75°C). Add cooking time if needed.
- Once the chicken is fully cooked, plate, serve, and enjoy!

PERUVIAN-STYLE CHICKEN WITH GREEN HERB SAUCE

Prep time: 15 minutes | Cook time: 15 minutes | Serves 4

Ingredients

For the Chicken:

- 1½ pounds (680 g) boneless, skinless chicken thighs
- 2 teaspoons grated lemon zest
- 2 tablespoons fresh lemon juice
- 1 tablespoon extra-virgin olive oil
- 1 serrano chile, seeded and minced
- 1 teaspoon ground cumin
- ½ teaspoon dried oregano, crushed
- ½ teaspoon kosher salt

For the Sauce:

- 1 cup fresh cilantro leaves
- 1 jalapeño, seeded and coarsely chopped
- 1 garlic clove, minced
- 1 tablespoon extra-virgin olive oil
- 2½ teaspoons fresh lime juice
- ¼ teaspoon kosher salt
- ⅓ cup mayonnaise
- Make the Chicken

Directions

- Use a fork to pierce the chicken all over to allow the marinade to penetrate better. In a small bowl, combine the lemon zest, lemon juice, olive oil, serrano, cumin, oregano, and salt. Place the chicken in a large bowl or large resealable plastic bag. Pour the marinade over the chicken. Toss to coat. Marinate at room temperature for 30 minutes, or cover and refrigerate for up to 24 hours.
- Place the chicken in the air-fryer cooking tray. (Discard remaining marinade.) Select Roast. Set temperature to 350°F (175°C), and set time to 15 minutes, turning halfway through the cooking time.
- Make the Sauce
- Meanwhile, combine the cilantro, jalapeño, garlic, olive oil, lime juice, and salt in a blender. Blend until combined. Add the mayonnaise and blend until pureed. Transfer to a small bowl. Cover and chill until ready to serve.

- At the end of the cooking time, use a meat thermometer to ensure the chicken has reached an internal temperature of 165°F (75°C). Serve the chicken with the sauce.
- Select Roast. Set temperature to 350°F (175°C). Set the timer and cook for 20 minutes.
- Using tongs, flip the turkey.
- Reset the timer and roast the turkey breast for another 30 minutes. Check that it has reached an internal temperature of 165°F (75°C). Add cooking time if needed.
- Using tongs, remove the turkey from the oven and let it rest for about 10 minutes before carving.

ASIAN-STYLE DUCK BREAST

Prep time: 5 minutes | Cook time: 30 minutes | Serves 3

Ingredients

- 1 pound (454 g) duck breast
- 1 tablespoon Hoisin sauce
- 1 tablespoon Five-spice powder
- Sea salt and black pepper, to taste
- ¼ teaspoon ground cinnamon

Directions

- Pat the duck breasts dry with paper towels. Toss the duck breast with the remaining ingredients.
- Select Roast. Set temperature to 330°F (165°C), and set time to 15 minutes, turning them over halfway through the cooking time.
- Turn the heat to 350°F (175°C); continue to cook for about 15 minutes or until cooked through.
- Let it rest for 10 minutes before carving and serving. Bon appétit!

GLUTEN-FREE CHICKEN CUTLETS

Prep time: 15 min | Cook time: 17 min | Serves: 4

Ingredients

Basil Buttermilk Sauce

- Buttermilk: ½ cup
- Chopped fresh basil: 2 tbsp.
- Hot sauce, 2 dashes
- Mayonnaise: ½ cup
- Half lemon's juice
- Salt & black pepper, to taste

Chicken cutlets

- Butter: 1 tbsp.
- 4 chicken breasts, boneless & skinless
- Dried potato flakes: 1 cup
- Parmesan cheese: ½ cup, grated
- 2 eggs, whisked
- Salt: ½ tsp.
- Canola oil: 1 tbsp.

Directions

- In a bowl, add all ingredients of the sauce, whisk well and set it aside.
- Let the Breville Smart air fryer oven preheat to 400° F.
- Pound the chicken and season with salt and pepper.
- In the food processor, add potato flakes (¼ cup), make them into a powder, and take them out in a bowl.
- In a different bowl, add eggs. In another bowl, add the rest of the potato flakes, salt, cheese and pepper.
- Coat the chicken in flakes powder, then in egg and lastly in potato flakes.
- Oil spray the chicken and air fry for 5 to 8 minutes, flipping halfway through.
- Serve with basil sauce.

LEMON ROSEMARY CHICKEN

Prep time: 30 min | Cook time: 20 min | Serves: 2

Ingredients

For marinade

- Olive oil: ½ tbsp.
- Chicken: 2 ½ cups
- Ginger: 1 tsp., minced
- Soy sauce: 1 tbsp.

For the sauce

- Half lemon
- Fresh rosemary: ½ cup, chopped
- Honey: 3 tbsp.
- Oyster sauce: 1 tbsp.

Directions

- In a big mixing bowl, add the marinade ingredients with chicken, and mix well.
- Keep in the fridge for 30 minutes
- Let the air fry preheat to 390° F.
- Place the marinated chicken in the air fryer. Air fry for 6 minutes.
- Add all the sauces ingredients in a bowl and mix well except for lemon wedges.
- Brush the sauce over half-baked chicken add lemon juice on top.
- Cook for another 13 minutes, flip the chicken halfway through. Let the chicken evenly brown.
- Serve right away.

BACON-WRAPPED CHICKEN BREASTS

Prep time: 15 min | Cook time: 30 min | Serves: 3

Ingredients

- 3 chicken breasts skinless, boneless
- 1 tsp. lemon-pepper seasoning
- 3 slices Monterey Jack cheese
- 6 spears of fresh asparagus
- 9 slices bacon

Directions

- Preheat the air fryer to 350° F
- Dry the chicken bits with paper towels. With a sharp knife, cut horizontally through the centre, beginning at the thickest part and not across to the other side. Spread out the two sides as if they were a novel.
- Lemon-pepper seasoning should be used on both sides. Place 1 slice of cheese on each chicken breast. Arrange four asparagus spear halves on top of the cheese. Roll the chicken up and then over the cheese and asparagus to keep the stuffing within each roll. Wrap several pieces of bacon on each chicken breast and protect the overlap with wooden toothpicks.
- In the air fryer, put each bacon-wrapped breast and air fry for 15 minutes. On the other side, cook for another 15 minutes. Insert an instant-read thermometer into the middle of the chicken to check for doneness; it should read 165° F

TURKEY MEATBALLS

Prep time: 5 min | Cook time: 16 min | Serves: 4

Ingredients

- Moroccan spice: 1 tbsp.
- Coriander: 1 tbsp.
- Pepper & salt
- Leftover turkey: 30g
- Soft cheese: 30g
- Couscous: ½ cup
- Turkey stock: 30 ml
- Cooked vegetables: 150g
- Greek yogurt: 1 tbsp.
- Desiccated coconut: 20g
- Cumin: 1 tbsp.

Directions

- In the blender, put the cooked vegetables, turkey leg meat, Greek yogurt (soft cheese), turkey stock, and seasoning. Blend for some minutes or till the mixture resembles the thick.
- Move the blender ingredients into the mixing bowl, put in a couscous and combine well.
- Form the combination into balls and roll in desiccated coconut.
- Put in your air fryer oven for 16 minutes on 360° F and then serve.

CRISPY CRUNCHY CHICKEN TENDERS

Prep time: 5 min | Cook time: 10 min | Serves: 4

Ingredients

- 1 tsp. Paprika
- 1 tsp. Salt
- ¼ tsp. Pepper
- 4 cups Breadcrumbs
- 3 Uncooked Chicken Breasts
- 1 Egg
- 2 tbsp. Milk

Directions

- Preheat your air fryer to 350° F on the Air Fry setting.
- Chicken breasts should be cut into strips.
- In one mug, whisk together the milk and the egg.
- In a separate bowl, combine breadcrumbs, paprika, salt, and pepper.
- Dredge the chicken strips in the egg mixture, then the breadcrumbs.
- Arrange 1-inch apart on the pan.
- Cook for 10 minutes in the air, turning halfway through.
- Use a thermometer to check the temperature. Cook until the internal temperature reaches 165° F, then continue to cook for a few minutes longer until finished.

TERIYAKI WINGS

Prep time: 5 min | Cook time: 20 min | Serves: 4

Ingredients

- Chicken wings: 2 lbs.
- Teriyaki sauce: ½ cup
- Minced garlic: 2 tsp.
- Ground ginger: ¼ tsp.
- Baking powder: 2 tsp.

Directions

- Except for the baking powder, place all ingredients in a bowl and marinate for 1 hour in the refrigerator. Place wings into your air fryer oven basket and sprinkle with baking powder.
- Gently rub into wings. Cook at 400° F for 25 minutes. Shake the basket 2- or 3-times during cooking. Serve.

BEEF EMPANADAS

Prep time: 20 min | Cook time: 15 min | Serves: 15

Ingredients

- Puff pastry, as needed
- Egg wash

Filling

- Olive oil: 1 tbsp.
- 2 minced garlic cloves
- 1 yellow onion, diced
- Cumin: 1 tsp.
- Ground beef: 1 lb.
- Salt & black pepper, to taste
- Tomato paste: 1 tbsp.
- Monterey Jack: 1 ¼ cup, shredded
- Oregano: 1 tsp.
- Paprika: ½ tsp.
- Shredded cheddar: 1 ¼ cup
- Pickled jalapeños: ½ cup, chopped
- Tomatoes: ½ cup, chopped

Directions

- In a pan, sauté onion in oil for 5 minutes, add garlic and cook for 1 minute.
- Add beef and cook for 5 minutes, drain any liquids.
- Add tomato paste, cook for 1 minute. Add the rest of the ingredients, except for cheese, cook for 3 to 4 minutes.
- Turn off the heat and let it cool
- Cut the dough into 4.5 inches of circles, with a cookie cutter
- Add 2 tbsp. of beef mixture and cheese on the dough circles. Fold the circle in half, seal the edges with water.
- Brush the empanadas with egg wash.
- Air fry for 10 minutes.
- Serve with sour cream.

MOZZARELLA-STUFFED MEATBALLS

Prep time: 10 min | Cook time: 40 min | Serves: 4

Ingredients

- Dried oregano: 1 tsp.
- Ground beef: 1 lb.
- 1 egg
- Breadcrumbs: ½ cup
- Mozzarella: 3 oz., cut into 16 cubes
- Freshly grated Parmesan: ¼ cup
- Chopped fresh parsley: ¼ cup
- 2 minced garlic cloves
- Salt & black pepper, to taste

Directions

- In a bowl, add all ingredients, except for cheese cubes, mix and make into 2 tbsp. of meal balls, flatten into patties.
- In each patty, add one cube and make it into a ball.
- Let the Breville Smart air fryer oven preheat to 370° F.
- Air fry the balls for 12 minutes, serve with marinara sauce.

BEEF WELLINGTON WONTONS

Prep time: 35 min | Cook time: 10 min | Serves: 24

Ingredients

- Olive oil: 1 tbsp.
- Lean ground beef: ½ lb.
- Butter: 1 tbsp.
- 2 minced garlic cloves
- Water: 1 tbsp.
- Dry red wine: ¼ cup
- Minced fresh parsley: 1 tbsp.
- Chopped shallot: 1 ½ tsp.
- Chopped different mushrooms: 3 cups
- Wonton wrappers: 12 oz., 1 pack
- Salt: ½ tsp.
- Pepper: ¼ tsp.
- 1 egg

Directions

- Let the Breville Smart air fryer oven preheat to 325° F.
- In a skillet, cook meat until no longer pink; for 4 to 5 minutes, take the beef out. Add butter, olive oil on medium flame. Add shallot, garlic, cook for 1 minute. Add wine and mushrooms. Cook for 8 to 10 minutes, until tender, add the beef back. Add parsley and salt, and black pepper.
- In every wonton wrapper, add some filling. Seal the edges with egg wash, and fold tightly.
- Oil spray the air fryer basket and air fry the wontons for 4 to 5 minutes, flip, oil spray and cook for 4 to 5 minutes, serve right away.

RIB EYE WITH HERB ROASTED MUSHROOMS

Prep time: 135 min | Cook time: 20 min | Serves: 4

Ingredients

- Worcestershire sauce: 2 tbsp.
- Thyme fresh leaves: 1 tsp.
- 2 rib-eye steaks, boneless
- Cremini mushrooms: 8 oz., without stems & caps halved
- Red wine: ¼ cup
- Olive oil: 2 tbsp.
- Salt & black pepper

Directions

- Season the steaks with black pepper.
- In a zip lock bag, add red wine and Worcestershire sauce. Mix and add steaks (pierce the steaks with a fork before adding to the bag). Keep in the fridge for 2 hours.
- Let the Breville Smart air fryer oven preheat to 400° F.
- In a bowl, add mushrooms, salt, pepper, olive oil, thyme, and parsley, toss to coat.
- Place the steaks in the air fryer basket, sprinkle salt and top with mushrooms.
- Air fry for ten-15 minutes. Flip halfway through.
- Serve with mushrooms and rice.

LAMB BURGERS

Prep time: 15 min | Cook time: 8 min | Serves: 6

Ingredients

- 2 lbs. ground lamb
- 1 tbsp. onion powder
- Salt and ground black pepper, as required

Directions

- In a bowl, add all the ingredients and mix well.
- Make 6 equal-sized patties from the mixture and arrange the patties onto a cooking tray.
- Arrange the drip pan in the bottom of air fryer oven cooking chamber.
- Take to the preheated air fryer at 360° F for 8 minutes. Turn the burgers after 4 minutes.
- When cooking time is complete, remove the tray from air fryer and serve hot.

SALT & PEPPER FILETS MIGNON

Prep time: 10 min | Cook time: 15 min | Serves: 4

Ingredients

- Kosher salt & coarse black pepper
- Filets mignons: 24 oz.

Horseradish sauce

- Prepared horseradish: 3 tbsp.
- Chopped fresh parsley: 1 tbsp.
- Sour cream: ¾ cup
- Lemon juice: 2 tbsp.
- Chopped fresh thyme: 1 tsp.

Directions

- Let the Breville Smart air fryer oven preheat to 400° F.
- Season the steaks with salt and pepper, and place in the air fryer.
- Air fry for 15 minutes, flipping halfway through.
- In a bowl, add all the ingredients of horseradish cream, mix and serve with steaks.

ZA'ATAR LAMB CHOPS

Prep time: 1 hour 5 min | Cook time: 10 min | Serves: 4

Ingredients

- Lamb loin chops: 8, trimmed.
- Black pepper
- Za'atar: 1 tbsp.
- Kosher salt: 1 ¼ tsp.
- Fresh lemon: ½
- Olive oil: 1 tsp.
- Garlic: 3 cloves, crushed.

Directions:

- Lamb chops rub with garlic and oil.
- Squash lemon on each side and season with za'atar, black pepper and salt.
- Preheat the air fryer at 400° F. Uneven layer and in batches cook to the desired, around 4 to 5 minutes on every side.
- On every bone, chops must have raw meat 2 ½ oz.

Prep time: 10 min | Cook time: 20 min | Serves: 4

Prep time: 15 min | Cook time: 10 min | Serves: 14

Ingredients

- Minced garlic: 2 cloves
- Italian seasoning: ½ tsp.
- Salt: ¾ tsp.
- Pepper: ¼ tsp.
- Ground beef: 1 lb.
- Dried breadcrumbs: ½ cup
- Parmesan cheese grated: ½ cup
- Milk: ¼ cup

Directions

- In the bowl, mix all the ingredients and form them into 1.5-inch meatballs.
- Place the meatballs in a single sheet into the air fryer basket without touching them.
- At 375° F, air fry your meatballs for 15 minutes.

Ingredients

- Sour cream: 1 cup
- Drained chopped green chills: 1 can
- Roll wrappers: 14
- Lightly beaten egg white: 1, large
- Cooking spray
- Salsa
- Ground beef: 1 lb.
- Chopped onion: 1 med.
- Taco seasoning: 1 envelope.
- Water: ¾ cup
- Shredded Monterey Jack cheese: 3 cups

Directions

- In the big skillet, cook beef and onion on med heat till meat is no further pink; drain. Stir in water and taco seasoning. Carry to a simmer. Lower the heat; boil, uncovered, for 5 minutes, stirring often. Take it from the heat; cool it lightly.
- Air fryer preheated to 375° F. In a big bowl, mix sour cream, chills and cheese. Whisk in beef combination. Put the egg roll wrapper on a work surface with one point facing you. Put ⅓ cup filling in the middle. Fold the bottom of ⅓ of the wrapper on filling; fold its insides.
- Coat the highest point with white egg; roll up to cover. Repeat with leftover wrappers and filling.
- In the batches, put chimichangas in the single layer on an oiled tray in the air fryer basket, Drizzle with cooking spray. Cook till golden brown for 3 to 4 minutes on both sides. Serve hot with salsa and extra sour cream.

RACK OF LAMB

Prep time: 5 min | Cook time: 15 min | Serves: 4

Ingredients

- 2 tsp. minced garlic
- Salt
- Pepper
- 4 tbsp. olive oil
- 1 rack of lamb
- 2 tbsp. dried rosemary dried thyme

Directions

- By combining the rosemary, thyme, garlic, salt, pepper, and olive oil in a small mixing bowl.
- Make a good mix.
- Then coat the lamb with the mixture.
- In an air fryer, position the rack of lamb.
- Preheat the air fryer to 360° F and keep it there for 10 minutes.
- After 10 minutes, use the method mentioned above to check the internal temperature of the rack of lamb.
- 150° F is rare.
- Then take it out, and serve

EASY ROSEMARY LAMB CHOPS

Prep time: 10 min | Cook time: 6 min | Serves: 4

Ingredients

- 4 lamb chops
- 2 tbsp dried rosemary
- ¼ cup fresh lemon juice
- Pepper
- Salt

Directions

- In a small bowl, mix together lemon juice, rosemary, pepper, and salt.
- Brush lemon juice rosemary mixture over lamb chops.
- Place lamb chops on air fryer oven tray and air fry at 400° F for 3 minutes.
- Turn lamb chops to the other side and cook for 3 minutes more.
- Serve and enjoy.

BEEF JERKY

Prep time: 10 min | Cook time: 4 hours | Serves: 4

Ingredients

- 2 lbs. London broil, sliced thinly
- 1 tsp. onion powder
- 3 tbsp. brown sugar
- 3 tbsp. soy sauce
- 1 tsp. olive oil

Directions

- Add all ingredients except meat in the large zip-lock bag.
- Mix until well combined. Add meat in the bag.
- Seal bag and massage gently to cover the meat with marinade.
- Let marinate the meat for 1 hour.
- Arrange marinated meat slices on air fryer tray and dehydrate at 160° F for 4 hours.

AIR FRYER MEATLOAF

Prep time: 10 min | Cook time: 25 min | Serves: 4

Ingredients

- 1 lb. lean beef
- 1 lightly beaten egg

- 3 tbsp. breadcrumbs
- 1 small, finely chopped onion
- 1 tbsp. chopped fresh thyme
- 1 tsp. salt
- 1 pinch ground black pepper to taste
- 2 thickly sliced mushrooms
- 1 tbsp. olive oil

Directions

- Preheat an air fryer up to 390° F.
- In a bowl, combine ground beef, egg, breadcrumbs, ointment, thyme, salt, and pepper. Knead and mix well.
- Move the mixture of beef into a baking pan and smooth the rim—press chestnuts into the top and coat with olive oil. Place the saucepan in the basket of the air fryer and slide into your air fryer oven.
- Set 25-minute air fryer timer and roast meatloaf until well browned.
- Set aside the meatloaf for at least 10 minutes before slicing and serving into wedges.

NEW YORK STRIP STEAK

Prep time: 5 minutes | Cook time: 15 minutes | Serves 4

Ingredients

- 1½ pounds (680 g) New York strip steak
- 2 tablespoons butter, melted
- Sea salt and ground black pepper, to taste
- 1 teaspoon paprika
- 1 teaspoon dried thyme
- 1 teaspoon dried rosemary

Directions

- Toss the beef with the remaining ingredients; place the beef in the Air Fryer cooking tray.
- Select Roast. Set temperature to 400ºF (205ºC), and set time to 15 minutes, turning it over halfway through the cooking time.
- Enjoy!

PULLED BEEF

Prep time: 10 minutes | Cook time: 1¼ hours | Serves 4

Ingredients

- 1½ pounds (680 g) beef brisket
- 2 tablespoons olive oil
- 3 garlic cloves, pressed
- Sea salt and ground black pepper, to taste
- 1 teaspoon red pepper flakes, crushed
- 2 tablespoons tomato ketchup
- 2 tablespoons Dijon mustard

Directions

- Toss the beef brisket with the olive oil, garlic, salt, black pepper, and red pepper; now, place the beef brisket in the Air Fryer cooking tray.
- Select Roast. Set temperature to 390ºF (200ºC) and set time to 15 minutes. Turn the beef over and reduce the temperature to 360ºF (180ºC).
- Continue to cook the beef brisket for approximately 55 minutes or until cooked through.
- Shred the beef with two forks; add in the ketchup and mustard and stir to combine well. Bon appétit!

COPYCAT TACO BELL CRUNCH WRAPS

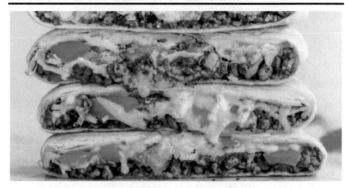

Prep time: 10 minutes | Cook time: 2 minutes | Serves 6

Ingredients

- 6 wheat tostadas
- 2 cups sour cream
- 2 cups Mexican blend cheese
- 2 cups shredded lettuce
- 12 ounces (340 g) low-sodium nacho cheese
- 3 Roma tomatoes
- 6 (12-inch) wheat tortillas
- 1⅓ cups water
- 2 packets low-sodium taco seasoning
- 2 pounds (907 g) of lean ground beef

Directions

- Ensure your air fryer oven is preheated to 400ºF (205ºC).
- Make beef according to taco seasoning packets.
- Place ⅔ cup prepared beef, 4 tablespoons nacho cheese, 1 tostada, ⅓ cup sour cream, ⅓ cup lettuce, ⅙ of tomatoes and ⅓ cup Mexican cheese on each tortilla.
- Fold up tortillas' edges and repeat with the remaining ingredients.
- Lay the folded sides of tortillas down into the oven and spray with olive oil.
- Select Roast. Set temperature to 400ºF (205ºC), and set time to 2 minutes.

PORK SPARERIBS

Prep time: 10 minutes | Cook time: 35 minutes | Serves 4

Ingredients

- 2 pounds (907 g) pork spareribs
- 1 teaspoon coarse sea salt
- ⅓ teaspoon freshly ground black pepper
- 1 tablespoon brown sugar
- 1 teaspoon cayenne pepper
- 1 teaspoon garlic powder
- 1 teaspoon mustard powder

Directions

- Toss all ingredients in a lightly greased Air Fryer cooking tray.
- Select Roast. Set temperature to 350ºF (175ºC), and set time to 35 minutes, turning them over halfway through the cooking time.
- Bon appétit!
- and croutons.
- Bon appétit!

ROSEMARY PORK BUTT

Prep time: 5 minutes | Cook time: 55 minutes | Serves 4

Ingredients

- 1½ pounds (680 g) pork butt
- 1 teaspoon butter, melted
- 2 garlic cloves, pressed
- 2 tablespoons fresh rosemary, chopped
- Coarse sea salt and freshly ground black pepper, to taste

Directions

- Toss all ingredients in a lightly greased Air Fryer cooking tray.
- Select Roast. Set temperature to 360ºF (180ºC), and set time to 55 minutes, turning it over halfway through the cooking time.
- Serve warm and enjoy!

HOT ST. LOUIS-STYLE RIBS

Prep time: 5 minutes | Cook time: 35 minutes | Serves 4

Ingredients

- 1½ pounds (680 g) St. Louis-style ribs
- 1 teaspoon hot sauce
- 1 tablespoon canola oil
- Kosher salt and ground black pepper, to taste
- 2 garlic cloves, minced

Directions

- Toss all ingredients in a lightly greased Air Fryer cooking tray.
- Select Roast. Set temperature to 350ºF (175ºC), and set time to 35 minutes, turning them over halfway through the cooking time.
- Bon appétit!

BREADED SIRLOIN CHOPS

Prep time: 10 minutes | Cook time: 15 minutes | Serves 3

Ingredients

- 1 pound (454 g) sirloin chops
- 1 egg
- 2 tablespoons butter, at room temperature
- Sea salt and ground black pepper, to taste
- 3 tablespoons Pecorino cheese, grated
- ½ cup breadcrumbs
- 1 teaspoon paprika
- 1 teaspoon garlic powder

Directions

- Pat the pork sirloin chops dry with kitchen towels.
- In a shallow bowl, whisk the egg until pale and frothy.
- In another shallow bowl, thoroughly combine the remaining ingredients. Dip the pork chops into the egg, then the cheese/crumb mixture.
- Place the pork sirloin chops in a lightly oiled Air Fryer cooking tray.
- Select Roast. Set temperature to 400ºF (205ºC), and set time to 15 minutes, turning them over halfway through the cooking time.
- Bon appétit!

BUTTERY ROSEMARY PORK LOIN ROAST

Prep time: 5 minutes | Cook time: 55 minutes | Serves 4

Ingredients

- 1½ pounds (680 g) pork loin roast
- 2 tablespoons butter, melted
- Sea salt and ground black pepper, to taste
- 1 teaspoon cayenne pepper
- 1 teaspoon garlic, pressed
- 1 teaspoon dried rosemary

Directions

- Toss all ingredients in a lightly greased Air Fryer cooking tray.
- Select Roast. Set temperature to 360°F (180°C), and set time to 55 minutes, turning it over halfway through the cooking time.
- Serve warm and enjoy!

PORK BULGOGI

Prep time: 15 minutes | Cook time: 15 minutes | Serves 4

Ingredients

- 1 onion, thinly sliced
- 2 tablespoons gochujang (Korean red chile paste)
- 1 tablespoon minced fresh ginger
- 1 tablespoon minced garlic
- 1 tablespoon soy sauce
- 1 tablespoon Shaoxing wine (rice cooking wine)
- 1 tablespoon toasted sesame oil
- 1 teaspoon sugar
- ¼ to 1 teaspoon cayenne pepper or gochugaru (Korean ground red pepper)
- 1 pound (454 g) boneless pork shoulder, cut into ½-inch-thick slices
- 1 tablespoon sesame seeds
- ¼ cup sliced scallions

Directions

- In a large bowl, combine the onion, gochujang, ginger, garlic, soy sauce, wine, sesame oil, sugar, and cayenne. Add the pork and toss to coat. Marinate at room temperature for 30 minutes or cover and refrigerate for up to 24 hours.
- Arrange the pork and onion slices in the air-fryer cooking tray; discard the marinade. Select Roast. Set temperature to 400°F (205°C), and set time to 15 minutes, turning the pork halfway through the cooking time.
- Arrange the pork on a serving platter. Sprinkle with the sesame seeds and scallions and serve.

PORK TAQUITOS

Prep time: 5 minutes | Cook time: 10 minutes | Serves 8

Ingredients

- 1 juiced lime
- 10 whole-wheat tortillas
- 2½ cups shredded Mozzarella cheese
- 30 ounces (850.5 g) of cooked and shredded pork tenderloin

Directions

- Ensure your air fryer oven is preheated to 380°F (195°C).
- Drizzle pork with lime juice and gently mix.
- Heat up tortillas in the microwave with a dampened paper towel to soften.
- Add about 3 ounces of pork and ¼ cup of shredded cheese to each tortilla. Tightly roll them up.
- Spray the air fryer cooking tray with a bit of olive oil.
- Select Roast, and set time to 7 to 10 minutes till tortillas turn a slight golden color, making sure to flip halfway through cooking process.

BRATWURST WITH BRUSSELS SPROUTS

Prep time: 10 minutes | Cook time: 15 minutes | Serves 4

Ingredients

- 1 pound (454 g) bratwurst
- 1 pound (454 g) Brussels sprouts
- 1 large onion, cut into wedges
- 1 teaspoon garlic, minced
- 1 tablespoon mustard
- 2 tablespoons honey

Directions

- Toss all Ingredients in a lightly greased Air Fryer cooking tray.
- Select Roast. Set temperature to 380°F (195°C), and set time to approximately 15 minutes, tossing the cooking tray halfway through the cooking time.
- Bon appétit!

DIJON PORK LOIN

Prep time: 10 minutes | Cook time: 55 minutes | Serves 4

Ingredients

- 1½ pounds (680 g) pork top loin
- 1 tablespoon olive oil
- 1 tablespoon Dijon mustard
- 2 cloves garlic, crushed
- 1 tablespoon parsley
- 1 tablespoon coriander
- ½ teaspoon red pepper flakes, crushed
- Kosher salt and ground black pepper, to taste

Directions

- Toss all Ingredients in a lightly greased Air Fryer cooking tray.
- Select Roast. Set temperature to 360°F (180°C), and set time to 55 minutes, turning it over halfway through the cooking time.
- Serve warm and enjoy!

SRIRACHA COUNTRY-STYLE RIBS

Prep time: 5 minutes | Cook time: 35 minutes | Serves 5

Ingredients

- 2 pounds (907 g) Country-style ribs
- ¼ cup Sriracha sauce
- 2 tablespoons bourbon
- 1 tablespoon honey
- 1 teaspoon stone-ground mustard

Directions

- Toss all Ingredients in a lightly greased Air Fryer cooking tray.
- Select Roast. Set temperature to 350ºF (175ºC), and set time to 35 minutes, turning them over halfway through the cooking time.
- Bon appétit!

PORK CHOPS WITH ORANGE GLAZE

Prep time: 5 minutes | Cook time: 15 minutes | Serves 3

Ingredients

- 1 pound (454 g) rib pork chops
- ½ tablespoon butter, melted
- 2 tablespoons orange juice, freshly squeezed
- 1 teaspoon rosemary, chopped
- Sea salt and cayenne pepper, to taste

Directions

- Toss all Ingredients in a lightly greased Air Fryer cooking tray.
- Select Roast. Set temperature to 400ºF (205ºC), and set time to 15 minutes, turning them over halfway through the cooking time.
- Bon appétit!

BUTTERY COUNTRY-STYLE RIBS

Prep time: 10 minutes | Cook time: 35 minutes | Serves 5

Ingredients

- 2 pounds (907 g) Country-style ribs
- Coarse sea salt and ground black pepper, to taste
- 1 teaspoon smoked paprika
- 1 teaspoon mustard powder
- 1 tablespoon butter, melted
- 1 teaspoon chili sauce
- 4 tablespoons dry red wine

Directions

- Toss all Ingredients in a lightly greased Air Fryer cooking tray.
- Select Roast. Set temperature to 350ºF (175ºC), and set time to 35 minutes, turning them over halfway through the cooking time.
- Bon appétit!

PORK CHOPS WITH WORCESTERSHIRE SAUCE

Prep time: 5 minutes | Cook time: 16 minutes | Serves 2

Ingredients

- 2 (10 ounce / 283-g) bone-in, center-cut pork chops, 1-inch thick
- 2 teaspoons Worcestershire sauce
- Salt and pepper, to taste
- Cooking spray

Directions

- Rub the Worcestershire sauce into both sides of pork chops.
- Season with salt and pepper to taste.
- Spray air fryer cooking tray with cooking spray and place the chops in cooking tray side by side.
- Select Roast. Set temperature to 360ºF (180ºC), and set time to 16 to 20 minutes or until well done. Let it rest for 5 minutes before serving.

Prep time: 25 min | Cook time: 20 min | Serves: 5-6

Ingredients

- Crushed pineapple unsweetened: ½ cup, with liquid
- Cider vinegar: ½ cup
- Packed dark brown sugar: ¼ cup
- 1 ¾ lbs., pork tenderloin, cut in half
- Ketchup: ¼ cup
- Sugar: ¼ cup
- Soy sauce: 1 tbsp.
- Dijon mustard: 1 ½ tsp.
- Garlic powder: ½ tsp.
- Salt & Pepper: ⅛ tsp. each

Directions

- In a saucepan, add all ingredients except for the pork. Let it come to a boil, turn the heat to a low simmer for 6 to 8 minutes.
- Let the Breville Smart air fryer oven preheat to 350° F.
- Season the pork with salt and pepper. Oil spray the pork and air fry for 7 to 8 minutes.
- Flip, add 2 tbsp. of sauce over pork cook for 10 to 12 minutes, until the internal temperature reaches 145° F.
- Rest it for 5 minutes, slice and serve with sauce.

Prep time: 10 minutes | Cook time: 14 minutes | Serves 4

Ingredients

- 4 thin boneless pork loin chops
- 2 tablespoons lemon juice
- ½ cup flour
- 1 teaspoon salt
- ¼ teaspoon marjoram
- 1 cup plain breadcrumbs
- 2 eggs, beaten
- Oil for misting or cooking spray
- lemon wedges

Directions

- Rub the lemon juice into all sides of pork chops.
- Mix together the flour, salt, and marjoram.
- Place flour mixture on a sheet of wax paper.
- Place breadcrumbs on another sheet of wax paper.
- Roll pork chops in flour, dip in beaten eggs, then roll in breadcrumbs. Mist all sides with oil or cooking spray.
- Spray air fryer cooking tray with nonstick cooking spray and place pork chops in cooking tray.
- Select Roast. Set temperature to 390°F (200°C), and set time to 7 minutes. Turn, mist again, and cook for another 7 or 8 minutes, until well done. Serve with lemon wedges.

STUFFED PORK CHOPS

Prep time: 40 min | Cook time: 20 min | Serves: 4

Ingredients

- Olive oil: ½ tsp.
- Chopped onion: ¼ cup
- Rubbed sage: ⅛ tsp.
- Bread: 4 slices, cubed
- 1 celery rib, diced
- Fresh parsley: 2 tbsp., chopped
- Salt: ⅛ tsp.
- White pepper: ⅛ tsp.
- Chicken broth: ⅓ cup
- Dried marjoram: ⅛ tsp.
- Dried thyme: ⅛ tsp.

Pork chops

- 4 pork rib chops
- Salt & pepper: ¼ tsp. each

Directions

- In a skillet, add oil, onion and celery and cook for 4 to 5 minutes. Turn off the heat.
- In a bowl, add seasonings and bread, broth and celery mixture. Mix well.
- Make a deep pocket in each pork chop, stuff with the celery mixture and secure with toothpicks.
- Let the Breville Smart air fryer oven preheat to 325° F.
- Season the chops with salt and pepper.
- Air fry the chops for 10 minutes, flip and cook for 5 to 8 minutes until the internal temperature of the meat reaches 165° F.

JERK PORK

Prep time: 4hours & 10min | Cook time: 20min | Serves: 4

Ingredients

- Jerk paste: ¼ cup
- Pork butt: 1.5 lbs., cut into 3" pieces

Directions

- Coat the pork well in the jerk paste and let it marinate for 4 to 24 hours in the fridge.
- Let the Breville Smart air fryer oven preheat to 390° F. Oil spray the basket of the air fryer.
- Let the pork come to room temperature before cooking, air fry for 20 minutes, flipping halfway through.
- Slice and serve

ASPARAGUS WITH TARRAGON

Prep time: 5 minutes | Cook time: 5 minutes | Serves 4

Ingredients

- 1 (1-pound / 454-g) bunch asparagus, washed and trimmed
- ⅛ teaspoon dried tarragon, crushed
- Salt and pepper, to taste
- 1 to 2 teaspoons extra-light olive oil

Directions

- Spread asparagus spears on cookie sheet or cutting board.
- Sprinkle with tarragon, salt, and pepper.
- Drizzle with 1 teaspoon of oil and roll the spears or mix by hand. If needed, add up to 1 more teaspoon of oil and mix again until all spears are lightly coated.
- Place spears in air fryer cooking tray. If necessary, bend the longer spears to make them fit. It doesn't matter if they don't lie flat.
- Select Broil. Set temperature to 390°F (200°C), and set time to 5 minutes. Shake air fryer cooking tray or stir spears with a spoon.
- Cook for an additional 4 to 5 minutes or just until crisp-tender.

CHEDDAR POTATO POT

Prep time: 10 minutes | Cook time: 15 minutes | Serves 4

Ingredients

- 3 cups cubed red potatoes (unpeeled, cut into ½-inch cubes)
- ½ teaspoon garlic powder
- Salt and pepper, to taste
- 1 tablespoon oil
- Chopped chives for garnish (optional)

For the Sauce:

- 2 tablespoons milk
- 1 tablespoon butter
- 2 ounces (57 g) sharp Cheddar cheese, grated
- 1 tablespoon sour cream

Directions

- Place potato cubes in large bowl and sprinkle with garlic, salt, and pepper. Add oil and stir to coat well.
- Select Roast. Set temperature to 390°F (200°C) and set time to 13 to 15 minutes or until potatoes are tender. Stir every 4- or 5-minutes during cooking time.
- While potatoes are cooking, combine milk and butter in a small saucepan. Warm over medium-low heat to melt butter.

Add cheese and stir until it melts. The melted cheese will remain separated from the milk mixture. Remove from heat until potatoes are done.

- When ready to serve, add sour cream to cheese mixture and stir over medium-low heat just until warmed. Place cooked potatoes in a serving bowl. Pour sauce over potatoes and stir to combine.
- Garnish with chives if desired.

OKRA

Prep time: 5 minutes | Cook time: 12 minutes | Serves 4

Ingredients

- 7 to 8 ounces (198 to 227 g) fresh okra
- 1 egg
- 1 cup milk
- 1 cup breadcrumbs
- ½ teaspoon salt
- Oil for misting or cooking spray

Directions

- Remove stem ends from okra and cut in ½-inch slices.
- In a medium bowl, beat together egg and milk. Add okra slices and stir to coat.
- In a sealable plastic bag or container with lid, mix together the breadcrumbs and salt.
- Remove okra from egg mixture, letting excess drip off, and transfer into bag with breadcrumbs.

- Shake okra in crumbs to coat well.
- Place all of the coated okra into the air fryer cooking tray and mist with oil or cooking spray. Okra doesn't need to cook in a single layer, nor is it necessary to spray all sides at this point. A good spritz on top will do.
- Select Roast. Set temperature to 390ºF (200ºC), and set time to 5 minutes. Shake the cooking tray to redistribute and give it another spritz as you shake.
- Cook for 5 more minutes. Shake and spray again. Cook for 2 to 5 minutes longer or until golden brown and crispy.

SPICED GLAZED CARROT

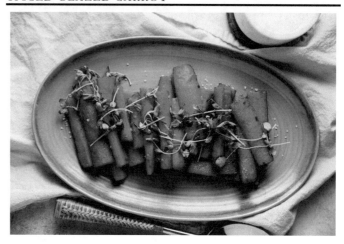

Prep time: 10 minutes | Cook time: 30 minutes | Serves 4

Ingredients

- Vegetable oil spray
- 4 cups frozen sliced carrots (do not thaw)
- 2 tablespoons brown sugar
- 2 tablespoons water
- ½ teaspoon ground cumin
- ½ teaspoon ground cinnamon
- ¼ teaspoon kosher salt
- 2 tablespoons coconut oil
- Chopped fresh parsley, for garnish

Directions

- Spray a 6 × 4-inch round heatproof pan with vegetable oil spray.
- In a medium bowl, combine the carrots, brown sugar, water, cumin, cinnamon, and salt. Toss to coat. Transfer to the prepared pan. Dot the carrots with the coconut oil, distributing it evenly across the pan. Cover the pan with foil.
- Place the pan in the air fryer cooking tray. Select Roast. Set temperature to 400ºF (205ºC), and set time to 10 minutes. Remove the foil and stir well. Place the uncovered pan back in the oven. Select Roast. Set temperature to 400ºF (205ºC), and set time to 20 minutes, or until the glaze is bubbling and the carrots are cooked through.
- Garnish with parsley and serve.

GOBI MANCHURIAN

Prep time: 15 minutes | Cook time: 20 minutes | Serves 4

Ingredients

For the Cauliflower:

- 4 cups chopped cauliflower
- 1 cup chopped yellow onion
- 1 large bell pepper, chopped
- 2 tablespoons vegetable oil
- 2 teaspoons kosher salt
- 1 teaspoon ground turmeric

For the Sauce:

- 3 tablespoons ketchup
- 2 tablespoons soy sauce
- 1 tablespoon rice vinegar
- 1 teaspoon minced garlic
- 1 teaspoon minced fresh ginger
- 1 teaspoon sriracha or other hot sauce
- Make the Cauliflower

Directions

- In a large bowl, combine the cauliflower, onion, and bell pepper. Drizzle with the vegetable oil and sprinkle with the salt and turmeric. Stir until the cauliflower is well coated.
- Place the cauliflower in the air-fryer cooking tray. Select Roast. Set temperature to 400ºF (205ºC), and set time to 20 minutes, stirring the cauliflower halfway through the cooking time.

Make the Sauce

- In a small bowl, combine the ketchup, soy sauce, vinegar, garlic, ginger, and sriracha.
- Transfer the cauliflower to a large bowl. Pour the sauce over and toss well to combine. Serve immediately.

LATKES WITH SOUR CREAM AND APPLESAUCE

Prep time: 10 minutes | Cook time: 12 minutes | Makes 12 latkes

Ingredients

- 1 russet potato
- ¼ onion
- 2 eggs, lightly beaten
- ⅓ cup flour
- ½ teaspoon baking powder
- 1 teaspoon salt
- Freshly ground black pepper, to taste
- Canola or vegetable oil, in a spray bottle
- Chopped chives, for garnish
- Apple sauce
- Sour cream

Directions

- Shred the potato and onion with a coarse box grater or a food processor with the shredding blade. Place the shredded vegetables into a colander or mesh strainer and squeeze or press down firmly to remove the excess water.
- Transfer the onion and potato to a large bowl and add the eggs, flour, baking powder, salt and black pepper. Mix to combine and then shape the mixture into patties, about ¼-cup of mixture each. Brush or spray both sides of the latkes with oil.
- Preheat the oven to 400ºF (205ºC).
- Roast the latkes in batches. Transfer one layer of the latkes to the air fryer cooking tray and select Roast. Set temperature to 400ºF (205ºC), and set time to 12 to 13 minutes, flipping them over halfway through the cooking time. Transfer the finished latkes to a platter and cover with aluminum foil, or place them in a warm oven to keep warm.
- Garnish the latkes with chopped chives and serve with sour cream and applesauce.

GREEN TOMATO WITH SRIRACHA MAYO

Prep time: 15 minutes | Cook time: 13 minutes | Serves 4

Ingredients

- 3 green tomatoes
- Salt and freshly ground black pepper, to taste
- ⅓ cup all-purpose flour
- 2 eggs
- ½ cup buttermilk
- 1 cup panko breadcrumbs
- 1 cup cornmeal
- Olive oil, in a spray bottle
- Fresh thyme sprigs or chopped fresh chives
- For the Sriracha Mayo:
- ½ cup mayonnaise
- 1 to 2 tablespoons sriracha hot sauce
- 1 tablespoon milk

Directions

- Cut the tomatoes in ¼-inch slices. Pat them dry with a clean kitchen towel and season generously with salt and pepper.
- Set up a dredging station using three shallow dishes. Place the flour in the first shallow dish, whisk the eggs and buttermilk together in the second dish, and combine the panko breadcrumbs and cornmeal in the third dish.
- Preheat the oven to 400ºF (205ºC).
- Dredge the tomato slices in flour to coat on all sides. Then dip them into the egg mixture and finally press them into the breadcrumbs to coat all sides of the tomato.
- Spray or brush the air-fryer cooking tray with olive oil. Transfer 3 to 4 tomato slices into the cooking tray and spray the top with olive oil. Select Roast. Set temperature to 400ºF (205ºC), and set time to 8 minutes. Flip them over, spray the other side with oil and roast for an additional 4 minutes until golden brown.
- While the tomatoes are cooking, make the sriracha mayo. Combine the mayonnaise, 1 tablespoon of the sriracha hot sauce and milk in a small bowl. Stir well until the mixture is smooth. Add more sriracha sauce to taste.

- When the tomatoes are done, transfer them to a cooling rack or a platter lined with paper towels so the bottom does not get soggy. Before serving, carefully stack the all the tomatoes into the oven and roast at 350ºF (175ºC), and set time to 1 to 2 minutes to heat them back up.
- Serve the fried green tomatoes hot with the sriracha mayo on the side. Season one last time with salt and freshly ground black pepper and garnish with sprigs of fresh thyme or chopped fresh chives.

SMASHED FRIED BABY RED POTATOES

Prep time: 10 minutes | Cook time: 18 minutes | Serves 3 to 4

Ingredients

- 1½ pounds (680 g) baby red or baby Yukon gold potatoes
- ¼ cup butter, melted
- 1 teaspoon olive oil
- ½ teaspoon paprika
- 1 teaspoon dried parsley
- Salt and freshly ground black pepper, to taste
- 2 scallions, finely chopped

Directions

- Bring a large pot of salted water to a boil. Add the potatoes and boil for 18 minutes or until the potatoes are fork-tender.
- Drain the potatoes and transfer them to a cutting board to cool slightly. Spray or brush the bottom of a drinking glass with a little oil. Smash or flatten the potatoes by pressing the glass down on each potato slowly. Try not to completely flatten the potato or smash it so hard that it breaks apart.
- Combine the melted butter, olive oil, paprika, and parsley together.
- Preheat the oven to 400ºF (205ºC).
- Spray the bottom of the air fryer cooking tray with oil and transfer one layer of the smashed potatoes into the cooking tray. Brush with some of the butter mixture and season generously with salt and freshly ground black pepper.
- Select Roast. Set temperature to 400ºF (205ºC), and set time to 10 minutes. Carefully flip the potatoes over and roast for an additional 8 minutes until crispy and lightly browned.

- Keep the potatoes warm in a 170ºF (75ºC) oven or tent with aluminum foil while you cook the second batch. Sprinkle minced scallions over the potatoes and serve warm.

CARIBBEAN YUCA ROOTS FRIES

Prep time: 5 minutes | Cook time: 25 minutes | Serves 4

Ingredients

- 3 yuca roots
- Vegetable oil for spraying
- 1 teaspoon kosher salt

Directions

- Trim the ends off the yuca roots and cut each one into 2 or 3 pieces depending on the length. Have a bowl of water ready. Peel off the rough outer skin with a paring knife or sharp vegetable peeler. Halve each piece of yuca lengthwise. Place the peeled pieces in a bowl of water to prevent them from oxidizing and turning brown.
- Fill a large pot with water and bring to a boil over high heat. Season well with salt. Add the yuca pieces to the water and cook until they are tender enough to be pierced with a fork, but not falling apart, approximately 12 to 15 minutes. Drain. Some of the yuca pieces will have fibrous string running down the center. Remove it. Cut the yuca into 2 or 3 pieces to resemble thick-cut french fries.
- Working in batches, arrange the yuca fries in rotisserie basket. Spray with oil. Select Roast. Set temperature to 400ºF (205ºC), and set time to 10 minutes, until the outside of the fries is crisp and browned and the inside fluffy. Repeat with the remaining fries. Spray the cooked yuca with oil and toss with 1 teaspoon salt.
- Serve the yuca fries warm with Toum, Chipotle Ketchup, or Mint Chimichurri.

FRIED RICE WITH SESAME-SRIRACHA SAUCE

Prep time: 10 min | Cook time: 20 min | Serves: 1-2

Ingredients

- Cooked white rice: 2 cups
- Salt & black pepper, to taste
- Sriracha: 1 tsp.
- Peas and carrots: 1 cup
- Toasted sesame oil: 2 tsp.
- Soy sauce: 1 tsp.
- Vegetable oil: 1 tbsp.
- Sesame seeds: ½ tsp.
- 1 egg, whisked

Directions

- In a bowl, add rice, sesame oil (1 tsp.), water (1 tbsp.), salt and pepper. Mix the rice.
- Transfer in a cake pan.
- Let the Breville Smart air fryer oven preheat to 350° F, cook the rice for 12 minutes, rotate halfway through.
- In a bowl, add sesame seeds, sriracha, sesame oil and soy sauce and mix.
- Pour over rice and air fry for 4 minutes, add carrots, peas, and egg. Mix and cook for 2 minutes more.
- Serve right away.

FRIED AVOCADO TACOS

Prep time: 30 min | Cook time: 20 min | Serves: 4

Ingredients

- Shredded coleslaw mix: 2 cups
- Minced fresh cilantro: ¼ cup
- Greek yogurt: ¼ cup
- Lime juice: 2 tbsp.
- Honey: 1 tsp.
- Salt: to taste
- Ground chipotle pepper: to taste
- Pepper: ¼ tsp.
- 1 egg, whisked
- Cornmeal: ¼ cup
- Garlic powder: ½ tsp.
- 2 avocados, sliced
- 8 tortillas (six inches)
- 1 tomato, chopped

Directions

- Let the Breville Smart air fryer oven preheat to 400° F.
- In a bowl, add the egg.
- In another bowl, add chipotle pepper, cornmeal, garlic powder and salt, mix.
- Coat the avocado slices in egg, then in cornmeal mixture. Oil spray the slices.
- Add the rest of the ingredients with chipotle pepper in a bowl, mix and keep in the fridge.
- Oil spray the air fryer basket, air fry the avocado slices for 4 minutes, flip, oil spray and cook for 3 to 4 minutes.
- Serve the slices in tortillas and salsa on top.

CAJUN FRIES

Prep time: 15 min | Cook time: 25 min | Serves: 4

Ingredients

- Cajun seasoning: 1 tbsp.
- 2 peeled Russet potatoes large, ½-inch sticks
- Canola oil: 2 tsp.

Cajun seasoning

- Dried thyme: ½ tsp.
- Salt: 2 tsp.
- Garlic powder: 1 tsp.
- Black pepper: 1 tsp.
- Cayenne pepper: 1 tsp.
- Paprika: 1 tsp.
- Dried oregano: ½ tsp.
- Onion powder: ½ tsp.

Directions

- Boil the potatoes for 4 minutes in salted boiling water.
- Take them out and wash with cold water, and pat dry.
- Let the Breville Smart air fryer oven preheat to 400° F.
- Toss the potatoes with oil and air fry for 25 minutes, shake the basket a few times.
- Sprinkle the Cajun seasoning on potatoes, oil spray and air fry for 5 minutes.
- Oil spray again and fry for 5 more minutes serve right away.

Prep time: 30 min | Cook time: 40 min | Serves: 4

Prep time: 30 min | Cook time: 10 min | Serves: 8

Ingredients

- Quinoa: 1 cup
- Water: 1 ½ cups
- Black pepper
- Rolled oats: 1 ½ cups
- Salt: 1 tsp.
- Chopped fresh chives: ¼ cup
- 3 eggs, whisked
- Minced onion: ¼ cup
- Crumbled feta cheese: ½ cup
- 4 buns

Ingredients

- Olive oil: 2 tbsp.
- Ricotta cheese: 4 oz.
- Large portobello mushrooms: 8 oz., without gills, finely chopped
- Dried oregano: 1 tsp.
- Red pepper flakes: ½ tsp.
- Salt: ¼ tsp.
- Dried thyme: 1 tsp.
- 1 pack of (8 oz.) cream cheese, softened
- 10 flour tortillas (8")

Directions

- Rinse and drain the quinoa, add in a pan, dry on medium flame. Add water, salt and pepper. Let it come to a boil, turn the heat low and simmer for 20-23 minutes.
- Turn off the heat, and cover with the lid. Spread on a sheet and cool.
- In a bowl, add onion, quinoa, herbs, oats, salt, cheese, pepper, and eggs. Mix and make into 4 patties; add some water if required.
- Oil sprays the patties and place them in the basket of the air fryer.
- Let the Breville Smart air fryer oven preheat to 400° F.
- Air fry the burgers for 10 minutes, flip halfway through.
- Serve in buns with desired toppings.

Directions

- Sauté mushrooms for four minutes, add herbs and spices. Cook for 4 to 6 minutes, turn off the heat and let it cool.
- In a bowl, add all cheeses, add mushrooms and mix.
- In each tortilla, add some mixture and roll tightly.
- Let the Breville Smart air fryer oven preheat to 400° F.
- Oil spray the tortillas and air fry for 9 to 11 minutes.
- Slice and serve.

CRISPY VEGETABLE QUESADILLAS

EGGPLANT PARMESAN

Prep time: 15 min | Cook time: 20 min | Serves: 4

Ingredients

- Canned black beans: 1 cup, rinsed
- Cheddar cheese, shredded: 1 cup
- 4 whole flour tortillas, (6")
- Fresh cilantro: 2 tbsp.
- Greek yogurt: 4 tbsp.
- Sliced zucchini: 1 cup
- Bell pepper, sliced: 1 cup
- 1 tsp. Lime zest & 1 tbsp. of lime juice
- ½ cup Pico de Gallo
- Ground cumin: ¼ tsp.

Directions

- Add 2 tbsp. of shredded cheese on half of each tortilla.
- Add black beans, pepper slices, zucchini slices, and more cheese.
- Fold the tortilla. Coat with oil spray and close with toothpicks.
- Oil spray the air fryer's basket. Place 2 quesadillas in the air fryer.
- Air fry for 10 minutes.
- In a bowl, mix yogurt, cumin, lime zest and lime juice.
- Slice and serve the quesadilla with sauce.

Prep time: 20 min | Cook time: 30 min | Serves: 6

Ingredients

- 1 Eggplant Medium sliced into ½-inch rounds
- ½ cup Italian breadcrumbs
- ¼ cup freshly grated Parmesan cheese
- 1 tsp. Italian seasoning
- 1 tsp. salt
- ½ tsp. basil
- ½ tsp. garlic
- ½ tsp. onion powder
- ½ tsp. black pepper
- ½ cup flour
- 1 egg beaten
- 1 cup marinara sauce or bolognas
- 6 slices mozzarella cheese, possibly more if you get more slices out of the eggplant

Directions

- Preheat the Air fryer oven on Air Fry mode to 360° F. The rack should be set to the middle position.
- Using a knife, cut the eggplant into ½-inch thick slices.
- Take three bowls and fill one with breadcrumbs and Parmesan cheese. In a separate bowl, whisk together the egg and milk. The third layer contains rice, salt, pepper, garlic, and onion powder.
- First, coat the sliced eggplant in flour, then in beaten eggs, and then in the bread crumb mixture.
- Enable to sit for a few minutes on the racks. Six should fit on 2 racks. Make certain they aren't in touch. You may need to do 2 batches.
- Cook for another 4 minutes before flipping. Depending on the thickness, an extra minute or two will be needed.
- 1 slice mozzarella cheese and marinara sauce on top of each eggplant round. Return to the air fryer for a minute or two more, or until the cheese has melted. If required, repeat with any remaining slices.

HOMEMADE PIZZA DOUGH

Prep time: 5 minutes | Cook time: 0 minutes | Makes 3 (6- to 8-ounce) dough balls

Ingredients

- 4 cups bread flour, pizza flour or all-purpose flour
- 1 teaspoon active dry yeast
- 2 teaspoons sugar
- 2 teaspoons salt
- 1½ cups water
- 1 tablespoon olive oil

Directions

- Combine the flour, yeast, sugar and salt in the bowl of a stand mixer. Add the olive oil to the flour mixture and start to mix using the dough hook attachment. As you're mixing, add 1¼ cups of the water, mixing until the dough comes together. Continue to knead the dough with the dough hook for another 10 minutes, adding enough water to the dough to get it to the right consistency.
- Transfer the dough to a floured counter and divide it into 3 equal portions. Roll each portion into a ball. Lightly coat each dough ball with oil and transfer to the refrigerator, covered with plastic wrap. You can place them all on a baking sheet, or place each dough ball into its own oiled zipper sealable plastic bag or container. (You can freeze the dough balls at this stage, removing as much air as possible from the oiled bag.) Keep in the refrigerator for at least one day, or as long as five days.
- When you're ready to use the dough, remove your dough from the refrigerator at least 1 hour prior to baking and let it sit on the counter, covered gently with plastic wrap.

PUMPKIN CINNAMON LOAF

Prep time: 15 minutes | Cook time: 20 minutes | Makes 1 loaf

Ingredients

- Cooking spray
- 1 large egg
- ½ cup granulated sugar
- ⅓ cup oil
- ½ cup canned pumpkin (not pie filling)
- ½ teaspoon vanilla
- ⅔ cup flour plus 1 tablespoon
- ½ teaspoon baking powder
- ½ teaspoon baking soda
- ½ teaspoon salt
- 1 teaspoon pumpkin pie spice
- ¼ teaspoon cinnamon

Directions

- Spray 6 × 6-inch baking dish lightly with cooking spray.
- Place baking dish in air fryer cooking tray and preheat air fryer oven to 330°F (165°C).
- In a large bowl, beat eggs and sugar together with a hand mixer.
- Add oil, pumpkin, and vanilla and mix well.
- Sift together all dry ingredients. Add to pumpkin mixture and beat well, about 1 minute.
- Pour batter in baking dish and select Bake, set the temperature to 330°F (165°C), and set the time to 20 minutes or until toothpick inserted in center of loaf comes out clean.

PARMESAN BREAD RING

Prep time: 10 minutes | Cook time: 30 minutes | Serves 6 to 8

Ingredients

- ½ cup unsalted butter, melted
- ¼ teaspoon salt (omit if using salted butter)
- ¾ cup grated Parmesan cheese
- 3 to 4 cloves garlic, minced
- 1 tablespoon chopped fresh parsley
- 1 pound (454 g) frozen bread dough, defrosted
- Olive oil
- 1 egg, beaten

Directions

- Combine the melted butter, salt, Parmesan cheese, garlic and chopped parsley in a small bowl.
- Roll the dough out into a rectangle that measures 8 inches by 17 inches. Spread the butter mixture over the dough, leaving a half-inch border un-buttered along one of the long edges. Roll the dough from one long edge to the other, ending with the un-buttered border. Pinch the seam shut tightly. Shape the log into a circle sealing the ends together by pushing one end into the other and stretching the dough around it.
- Cut out a circle of aluminum foil that is the same size as the air fryer cooking tray. Brush the foil circle with oil and place an oven-safe ramekin or glass in the center. Transfer the dough ring to the aluminum foil circle, around the ramekin. This will help you make sure the dough will fit in the cooking tray and maintain its ring shape. Use kitchen shears to cut 8 slits around the outer edge of the dough ring halfway to the center. Brush the dough ring with egg wash.
- Preheat the oven to 400°F (205°C) for 4 minutes. Brush the sides of the cooking tray with oil and transfer the dough ring, foil circle and ramekin into the cooking tray. Slide the drawer back into the oven, but do not turn the oven on. Let the dough rise inside the warm air fryer oven for 30 minutes.
- After the bread has proofed in the air fryer oven for 30 minutes, select Air Fry, set the temperature to 340°F (170°C), and set the time to 15 minutes. Flip the bread over by inverting it onto a plate or cutting board and sliding it back into the air fryer cooking tray. Air fry for another 15 minutes.

DOUBLE CHEESE SALAMI AND KALE PIZZA

Prep time: 10 minutes | Cook time: 8 minutes | Makes 1 pizza

Ingredients

- 4 ounces (113 g) pizza dough
- 2 teaspoons olive oil
- ¼ cup packed torn kale leaves
- 5 slices (1½ to 2 inch diameters) salami
- 3 tablespoons grated Asiago cheese
- 2 tablespoons shredded low-moisture Mozzarella cheese
- Kosher salt and freshly ground black pepper, to taste

Directions

- Roll and stretch the pizza dough into a 6-inch round.
- Lay the dough round in the air fryer, then brush with 1 teaspoon of the olive oil. Arrange the kale leaves over the dough, followed by the salami slices. Sprinkle with the Asiago and Mozzarella. Season with salt and pepper, drizzle with the remaining 1 teaspoon olive oil, and select Pizza, set the temperature to 350°F (177°C), and set the time to 8 minutes or until the dough is cooked through and the cheese is melted and golden brown.
- Transfer the pizza to a plate and serve hot.

SMOKED MOZZARELLA, MUSHROOM, AND THYME PIZZA

Prep time: 10 minutes | Cook time: 8 minutes | Makes 1 pizza

Ingredients

- 4 ounces (113 g) pizza dough
- 2 teaspoons olive oil
- ½ cup oyster mushrooms, torn into small pieces
- 1 teaspoon fresh thyme leaves
- ¼ cup shredded smoked Mozzarella cheese
- ⅛ teaspoon crushed red chile flakes

Directions

- Kosher salt and freshly ground black pepper, to taste
- Roll and stretch the pizza dough into a 6-inch round.
- Lay the dough round in the air fryer, then brush with 1 teaspoon of the olive oil. Arrange the mushrooms over the dough, followed by the thyme leaves. Sprinkle with the smoked Mozzarella and chile flakes. Season with salt and black pepper, drizzle with the remaining 1 teaspoon of olive oil, and select Pizza, set the temperature to 350ºF (180ºC), and set the time to 8 minutes or until the dough is cooked through and the cheese is melted and golden brown.
- Transfer the pizza to a plate and serve hot.

VEGAN CRUSHED TOMATO PIZZA

Prep time: 10 minutes | Cook time: 8 minutes | Makes 1 pizza

Ingredients

- 1 tablespoon walnut halves
- 1½ teaspoons nutritional yeast
- ½ teaspoon garlic powder
- 4 ounces (113 g) pizza dough
- 2 teaspoons olive oil
- 2 canned whole peeled tomatoes, crushed by hand and drained
- Kosher salt and freshly ground black pepper, to taste
- 1 tablespoon thinly sliced fresh flat-leaf parsley

Directions

- Set a Microplane grater over a small bowl and grate the walnuts into the bowl. Stir in the nutritional yeast and garlic powder. Roll and stretch the pizza dough into a 6-inch round.
- Lay the dough round in the air fryer cooking tray, then brush with 1 teaspoon of the olive oil. Arrange the crushed tomatoes over the dough and sprinkle with the walnut "Parmesan" mixture. Season with salt and pepper, drizzle with the remaining 1 teaspoon olive oil, and select Pizza, set the temperature to 350ºF (177ºC), and set the time to 8 minutes or until the dough is cooked through, the tomatoes are dried out, and the "Parmesan" is browned.
- Transfer the pizza to a plate, sprinkle with the parsley, and serve hot.

SWEET ROSEMARY KNOTS

Prep time: 15 minutes | Cook time: 14 minutes | Makes 8 garlic knots

Ingredients

- ¼ cup milk, heated to 115°F (46°C) in the microwave
- ½ teaspoon active dry yeast
- 1 tablespoon honey or agave syrup
- ⅔ cup all-purpose flour, plus more for dusting
- ½ teaspoon kosher salt
- 2 tablespoons unsalted butter, at room temperature, plus more for greasing and brushing
- 2 tablespoons olive oil
- 1 tablespoon finely chopped fresh rosemary
- 1 teaspoon garlic powder
- 2 garlic cloves, minced
- ¼ teaspoon freshly ground black pepper
- Flaky sea salt

Directions

- In a large bowl, whisk together the milk, yeast, and honey and let them stand until foamy, about 10 minutes. Stir in the flour and kosher salt until just combined. Stir in the butter until completely absorbed. Scrape the dough onto a lightly floured work surface and knead until smooth, for about 6 minutes. Transfer the dough to a bowl lightly greased with more butter, cover loosely with a sheet of plastic wrap or a kitchen towel, and let sit until nearly doubled in size, for about 1 hour.
- Uncover the dough, lightly press it down to expel the bubbles, then portion it into 8 equal pieces. Roll each piece into a 6-inch rope, then tie it into a simple knot, tucking the loose ends into each side of the "hoop" made by the knot. Return the knots to the bowl they proofed in, then add the olive oil, rosemary, garlic powder, fresh garlic, and pepper. Toss the knots until coated in the oil and spices, then nestle them side by side in the air fryer cooking tray. Cover the knots loosely with plastic wrap and let sit until lightly risen and puffed, for 20 to 30 minutes.
- Uncover the knots and select Bake, set the temperature to 280°F (138°C), and set the time to 14 minutes or until the knots are golden brown outside and tender and fluffy inside. Remove the garlic knots from the air fryer and brush with a little more butter, if you like, and sprinkle with a pinch of sea salt. Serve warm.

SAMOSA VEGGIE POT PIE

Prep time: 15 minutes | Cook time: 51 minutes | Serves 2

Ingredients

- 3 tablespoons vegetable oil
- 1 teaspoon brown mustard seeds
- 1 medium yellow onion, roughly chopped
- ½ to 1 serrano chile, seeded and minced
- 1 teaspoon garam masala
- 1 teaspoon ground coriander
- ½ teaspoon ground cumin
- ½ teaspoon ground turmeric
- ½ teaspoon sweet paprika
- 3 garlic cloves, minced
- 1 pound (454 g) russet potatoes, peeled, boiled, and cut into 1-inch chunks
- ½ cup thawed frozen peas
- 2 teaspoons fresh lemon juice
- Kosher salt and freshly ground black pepper, to taste
- All-purpose flour, for rolling/dusting
- 2 sheets puff pastry, thawed if frozen

Directions

- In a medium saucepan, heat the oil over medium-high heat. Add the mustard seeds and cook until they begin popping, for 1 to 1½ minutes. Add the onion and chile and cook, stirring, until soft and caramelized at the edges, for about 10 minutes.
- Add the garam masala, coriander, cumin, turmeric, paprika, and garlic and cook until fragrant, about 1 minute. Stir in the potatoes, peas, and lemon juice, breaking the potatoes up slightly and stirring until everything is coated in the yellow stain of the turmeric. Remove the pan from the heat, season the filling with salt and pepper, and let it cool completely. The filling can be made and stored in a bowl in the refrigerator for up to 3 days before you plan to cook the pie.
- Working on a lightly floured surface, roll 1 pastry sheet into a 10-inch square, then cut out a 10-inch round, discarding the scraps. Mound the cooled potato filling in the center of the dough round, then press and mold it with your hands into a 7-inch disk. Cut a 7-inch round out of the second pastry sheet (no need to roll) and place it over the filling disk. Brush the edge of the bottom dough round with water just to moisten,

then lift it up to meet the top dough round. Pinch and fold the edges together all around the filling to form and enclose the pie.

- Transfer the pie to the air fryer, and cut a slit in the top of the pie with a paring knife to vent. Cover the top of the pie loosely with a round of foil, and select Bake, set the temperature to 310ºF (155ºC), and set the time to 20 minutes. Remove the foil and bake at 330ºF (165ºC) until the pastry is golden brown and the filling is piping hot, about 20 minutes or more.

XL CHIMICHURRI BEEF EMPANADAS

Prep time: 10 minutes | Cook time: 24 minutes | Serves 2

Ingredients

- ½ pound (227 g) trimmed beef sirloin, cut into ½-inch pieces, at room temperature
- 1 tablespoon chopped fresh flat-leaf parsley leaves
- 1 tablespoon chopped fresh cilantro leaves
- 1 tablespoon chopped fresh mint leaves
- 1 tablespoon olive oil
- 2 teaspoons red wine vinegar
- ½ teaspoon kosher salt
- ¼ teaspoon ground cumin
- 2 garlic cloves, minced
- Freshly ground black pepper, to taste
- 12 ounces (340 g) pizza dough

Directions

- In a bowl, toss together the beef, parsley, cilantro, mint, olive oil, vinegar, salt, cumin, garlic, and pepper.
- Divide the dough in half and flatten each portion into a 10-inch round. Divide the beef mixture between the 2 dough rounds, then fold them in half to create 2 half-moons. Use a

fork or your fingers to crimp and twist the edges of the dough in on itself to seal the empanadas completely.

- Place one empanada in the air fryer cooking tray, cut a hole in the top with a paring knife to vent, and select Bake, set the temperature to 350ºF (175ºC), and set the time to 12 minutes or until the dough is golden brown and the beef is cooked through. Transfer the empanada to a plate and let it cool for 2 minutes before serving. Repeat for the second empanada.

BACON CHEESE PIZZA

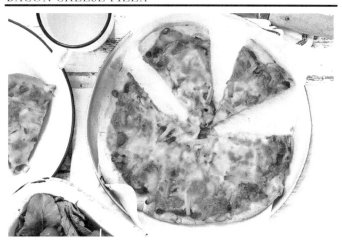

Prep time: 10 minutes | Cook time: 20 minutes | Serves 4

Ingredients

- Flour, for dusting
- Nonstick baking spray with flour
- 4 frozen large whole-wheat dinner rolls, thawed
- 5 cloves garlic, minced
- ¾ cup pizza sauce
- ½ teaspoon dried oregano
- ½ teaspoon garlic salt
- 8 slices precooked bacon, cut into 1-inch pieces
- 1¼ cups shredded Cheddar cheese

Directions

- On a lightly floured surface, press out each dinner roll to a 5-by-3-inch oval.
- Spray four 6-by-4-inch pieces of heavy-duty foil with nonstick spray and place one crust on each piece.
- Select Bake, cook for 2 minutes or until the crusts are set, but not browned.
- Meanwhile, in a small bowl, combine the garlic, pizza sauce, oregano, and garlic salt. When the pizza crusts are set, spread each with some of the sauce. Top with the bacon pieces and Cheddar cheese.
- Select Pizza, cook for 18 minutes or until the crust is browned and the cheese is melted and starting to brown.

BLT SANDWICH

Prep time: 10 minutes | Cook time: 10 minutes | Serves 3

Ingredients

- 6 ounces (170 g) bacon, thick-cut
- 2 tablespoons brown sugar
- 2 teaspoons chipotle chile powder
- 1 teaspoon cayenne pepper
- 1 tablespoon Dijon mustard
- 1 heads lettuce, torn into leaves
- 2 medium tomatoes, sliced
- 6 (½-inch) slices white bread

Directions

- Toss the bacon with the sugar, chipotle chile powder, cayenne pepper, and mustard.
- Place the bacon in the Air Fryer cooking tray. Then select Bake, set the temperature to 400°F (205°C), and set the time to 10 minutes, tossing the cooking tray halfway through the cooking time.
- Assemble your sandwiches with the bacon, lettuce, tomato and bread.
- Bon appétit!

MUSHROOM AND TOMATO PITA PIZZA

Prep time: 10 minutes | Cook time: 3 minutes | Serves 4

Ingredients

- 4 (3-inch) pitas
- 1 tablespoon olive oil
- ¾ cup pizza sauce
- 1 jar (4 ounces /113g) sliced mushrooms, drained
- ½ teaspoon dried basil
- 2 green onions, minced
- 1 cup grated Mozzarella or provolone cheese
- 1 cup sliced grape tomatoes

Directions

- Brush each piece of pita with oil and top with the pizza sauce.
- Add the mushrooms and sprinkle with basil and green onions. Top with the grated cheese.
- Select Pizza, and set the time to 3 to 6 minutes or until the cheese is melted and starts to brown. Top with the grape tomatoes and serve immediately.

Prep time: 5 minutes | Cook time: 10 minutes | Serves 2

Ingredients

- 4 slices sourdough bread
- 2 tablespoons butter, room temperature
- 4 slices Cheddar cheese
- ½ pound (227 g) corned beef

Directions

- Butter one side of each slice of bread.
- Assemble your sandwiches with cheese and corned beef.
- Select Air Fry, set the temperature to 380ºF (193ºC), and set the time to 10 minutes.
- Bon appétit!

Prep time: 5 minutes | Cook time: 12 minutes | Serves 4

Ingredients

- 1 pound (454 g) chicken breasts
- 1 tablespoon olive oil
- Sea salt and black pepper, to taste
- 4 slices Cheddar cheese
- 4 teaspoons yellow mustard
- 4 English muffins, lightly toasted

Directions

- Pat the chicken dry with kitchen towels. Toss the chicken breasts with the olive oil, salt, and pepper.
- Select Bake, set the temperature to 380ºF (193ºC), and set the time to 12 minutes, turning them over halfway through the cooking time.
- Shred the chicken using two forks and serve with cheese, mustard, and English muffins. Bon appétit!

PEANUT BUTTER BREAD

Prep time: 5 minutes | Cook time: 5 minutes | Serves 3

Ingredients

- 1 tablespoon oil
- 2 tablespoons peanut butter
- 4 slices bread
- 1 banana, sliced

Directions

- Spread the peanut butter on top of each slice of bread, then arrange the banana slices on top. Sandwich two slices together, then the other two.
- Bursh oil the inside of the Air Fryer cooking tray and select Bake, set the temperature to 300ºF (149ºC), and set the time to 5 minutes.
- Serve.

MAPLE BANANA CHIA BREAD

Prep time: 15 minutes | Cook time: 27 minutes | Serves 6

Ingredients

- 2 large bananas, very ripe, peeled
- 2 tablespoons neutral-flavored oil (sunflower or safflower)
- 2 tablespoons maple syrup
- ½ teaspoon vanilla
- ½ tablespoon chia seeds
- ½ tablespoon ground flaxseed
- 1 cup whole-wheat pastry flour
- ¼ cup coconut sugar
- ½ teaspoon cinnamon
- ¼ teaspoon salt
- ¼ teaspoon nutmeg
- ¼ teaspoon baking powder
- ¼ teaspoon baking soda

Directions

- Cooking oil spray (sunflower, safflower, or refined coconut)
- In a medium bowl, mash the peeled bananas with a fork until very mushy. Add the oil, maple syrup, vanilla, chia, and flaxseeds and stir well.
- Add the flour, sugar, cinnamon, salt, nutmeg, baking powder, and baking soda, and stir just until thoroughly combined.
- Preheat a 6-inch round, 2-inch deep baking pan in the oven for 2 minutes.
- Open the oven to spray the baking pan with oil, and pour the batter into it. Smooth out the top with a rubber spatula and select Bake, set the temperature to 350ºF (175ºC) and set the time to 25 minutes or until a knife inserted in the center comes out clean.
- Remove and cool for a minute or two, then cut into wedges and serve.

CHOCOLATE CHIP OATMEAL COOKIES

Prep time: 20 min | Cook time: 10 min | Serves: 24

Ingredients

- Butter: 1 cup, softened
- Sugar: ¾ cup
- Instant vanilla pudding mix: 1 pack, 3.4 oz.
- All-purpose flour: 1-½ cups
- 2 eggs
- Vanilla extract: 1 tsp.
- Packed brown sugar: ¾ cup
- Quick-cooking oats: 3 cups
- Semisweet chocolate chips: 2 cups
- Baking soda: 1 tsp.
- Salt: 1 tsp.
- Chopped nuts: 1 cup

Directions

- Let the Breville Smart air fryer oven preheat to 325° F.
- In a bowl, cream the sugars and butter for 5 to 7 minutes.
- Add vanilla and eggs.
- In a different bowl, add flour, baking soda, oats, pudding mix, salt. Mix and add into the creamed mix.
- Add nuts and chocolate chips.
- Place spoon full of dough on the air fryer tray bake for 8 to 10 minutes.
- Serve warm.

CRUSTLESS CHEESECAKE

Prep time: 10 min | Cook time: 10 min | Serves: 2

Ingredients

- Vanilla extract: 1 tsp.
- Sweetener: ¾ cup
- Sour cream: 2 tbsp.
- Cream cheese: 16 oz. Softened
- 2 eggs
- Lemon juice: ½ tsp.

Directions

- Let the Breville Smart air fryer oven preheat to 350° F.
- Add all the ingredients in the blender, pulse until smooth.
- Pour into two spring forms (4-inch), air fry for 8 to 10 minutes.
- Serve chilled.

RASPBERRY ALMOND FRUIT SQUARES

Prep time: 20 min | Cook time: 30 min | Serves: 8

Ingredients

- Almond paste: 2 oz.
- All-purpose flour: 1 cup
- Unsalted butter: ¼ cup, softened
- 1 egg
- Baking powder: ¼ tsp.
- Baking soda: ¼ tsp.
- Raspberries: 2 cups
- Sugar: ⅓ cup
- Raspberry jam: ⅓ cup
- Salt: ⅛ tsp.

Topping layer:

- Oatmeal: ⅓ cup
- Butter: 3 tbsp., melted
- Brown sugar: ⅓ cup
- All-purpose flour: ⅓ cup
- Sliced almonds: ⅓ cup

Directions

- Let the Breville Smart air fryer oven preheat to 350° F on Bake mode.
- Place parchment paper in the 7" cake pan.
- In a food processor, add butter and almond paste pulse to combine.
- Add egg, sugar, pulse until smooth.
- Add the rest of the ingredients until dough forms.
- Press this mixture in the lined cake pan.
- Bake for 10 minutes.
- Whisk the jam, add raspberries.
- Pour this mixture over the crust.
- In a bowl, add all the ingredients of toppings. Sprinkle all over the jam.
- Cover the pan with aluminium foil and bake for 10 minutes.
- Take the foil off and air fry for 10 more minutes.
- Serve warm.

PEANUT BUTTER DOUGHNUT HOLES

Prep time: 3 hours | Cook time: 5 min | Serves: 12

Ingredients

- Active dry yeast: 1 tsp.
- Salt: ¼ tsp.
- Warm milk: ½ cup
- 24 mini peanut butter cups
- Sugar: 1 tbsp.
- Vanilla extract: half tsp.
- Bread flour: 1½ cups
- 2 egg yolks
- Melted butter: 2 tbsp.

Directions

- In a bowl, add sugar, yeast and flour.
- Add butter, milk, egg yolks, and vanilla. Mix until dough forms. Knead with hands for 2 minutes.
- Place this dough in an oiled bowl and cover with a towel. Place in a warm place for 60-90 minutes.
- Make 24" log from the dough. Slice into 24 pieces.
- Add 1 piece of peanut butter cup in each dough piece and make it into a ball.
- Keep them in a warm place for half an hour.
- Let the Breville Smart air fryer oven preheat to 400° F.
- Oil spray the dough balls and air fry for four minutes, flip halfway through.
- Serve right away.

MINI LEMON TARTLETS

Prep time: 30 min | Cook time: 20 min | Serves: 12

Ingredients

- 1 box of lemon dessert mix
- Raspberries
- 12 mini tart shells

Directions

- Preheat the air fryer to 350° F on the Bake mode level.
- Make the dessert mix according to the product directions.
- On a shelf, place the mini tart shells.
- Bake for 1-2 minutes the empty mini tart shells. Don't overcook the food.
- Take the mini tart shells out of the air fryer and fill them with your dessert filling.
- Bake for 5 minutes filled mini-tarts. If you haven't finished yet, add a few minutes.
- Take out of the air fryer and set aside to cool.
- Serve with your favourite fruit (we used raspberries) and a dusting of icing sugar.

PEPPERMINT LAVA CAKE

Prep time: 5 min | Cook time: 25 min | Serves: 4

Ingredients

- 1 cup Confectioners' sugar
- ⅔ cup Semisweet chocolate chips
- 2 large Eggs
- 1 tsp. Peppermint extract
- 6 tbsp. All-purpose flour
- Butter: ½ cup

Directions

- Preheated air fryer to 375° F. In the microwave-safe bowl, melt butter and chocolate chips for about 30 seconds, whisk till smooth. Stir in the confectioners' sugar, egg yolks, eggs and extract till well blended. Fold in the flour.
- Gently oil and flour four ramekins put the batter into the ramekins. Don't overfill. On the tray in an air fryer, put ramekins; cook till the thermometer reaches 160° F and edges of cakes are set, 10 to 12 minutes.
- Take it from the; let it sit for five minutes. Safely run the knife around the sides of ramekins sometimes to loosen the cake, invert onto the dessert plates. Drizzle with the crushed candies. Now serve immediately.

CUPCAKES

Prep time: 20 min | Cook time: 12 min | Serves: 3-4

Ingredients

- 1 tbsp. Olive Oil
- Self-Raising Flour: 14 oz.
- Caster Sugar: 15.8 oz.
- 4 Eggs
- 1 tbsp. Vanilla Essence
- Butter room temperature: 7 oz.
- Skimmed Milk: 16.9 oz.

Chocolate Buttercream:

- 1 tbsp. Maple Syrup
- Butter: 8 oz.
- Cocoa Powder: 1.5 oz.
- 3 tbsp. Single Cream
- Icing Sugar: 14.8 oz.
- 2 tsp. Vanilla Essence

Directions

- Combine the butter and sugar in a mixing bowl and beat the butter into the sugar with a hand mixer. In a mixing bowl, break eggs, apply vanilla extract, extra virgin olive oil, and whisk again with a hand mixer. Mix in the cocoa powder, flour, and milk with a wooden spoon until it's creamy. Use a stand mixer instead of a hand mixer to avoid overmixing. Adjust the consistency with a little more skimmed milk or water if it's too thick.
- Fill muffin cups halfway with batter and bake for 12 minutes at 320° F in the air fryer. Place on a plate and set aside to cool.
- Make your chocolate buttercream as it cools. Mix the icing sugar into the butter with a hand mixer. Mix in the remaining ingredients until you have a creamy buttercream. Refrigerate your cupcakes while they cool.

- Make a fist with your piping bag from the bottom. Then open it up over your hand to form a funnel. Then spoon your mixture into the piping bag with your other hand. But first, make sure you've got the correct nozzle for piping; otherwise, you'll have to start over, which is a hassle. When the piping bag is nearly full, twist it close, gently squeeze to release some air, then squeeze with gentle pressure and swirl it on top.

CHOCOLATE HAZELNUT PASTRY

Prep time: 10 min | Cook time: 15 min | Serves: 4

Ingredients

- 1 tbsp. of water
- 2 tbsp. of turbinado sugar
- 4 tbsp. of hazelnut spread
- 4 tsp. slivered almonds plus more for garnish
- (8 oz.)1 layer frozen puff pastry
- 1 beaten egg

Directions

- On a lightly floured surface, thaw and open the puff pastry according to the package Directions.
- Break the puff pastry into four squares. Fill each square with a heaping tablespoon of hazelnut spread. Slivered almonds should be sprinkled on top.
- To make a rectangle, wet the edges of each pastry and fold them together. To seal the edges, use a fork to press them together.
- Combine the egg and 1 tbsp. of water in a small mixing cup. Apply the egg wash to the top of the puff pastry.
- Sprinkle the turbinado sugar over the pastries' tops. To finish, sprinkle a few slivered almonds on top of each pastry.
- Move the pastries to two baking trays with care.
- Place the drip pan in the cooking chamber's rim. Select Air Fry from the display panel then set the temperature to 330° F and the time to 10 minutes, then press START.
- Insert one cooking tray in the middle position and one tray in the bottom-most position when the show says "Add Food."
- When the show says "Switch Food," don't flip the food; instead, swap the cooking trays so that the one in the middle is now in the bottom-most position, and the one in the bottom-most position is now in the top-most position.

- Keep an eye on the pastries and take them out when they've turned a dark golden brown. Heat the dish before eating.

- Remove the apple fritters from the air fryer, put them on a wire rack, and drizzle the glaze over them right away

APPLE FRITTERS

Prep time: 10 min | Cook time: 6-7min | Serves: 4

Ingredients

- 1 tsp. baking powder
- 2 apples, cored and diced
- 1 cup all-purpose flour
- ½ tsp. salt
- ½ tsp. ground cinnamon
- ¼ tsp. ground nutmeg
- ⅓ cup milk
- 2 tbsp. butter, melted
- ½ tsp. lemon juice
- 1 egg

Cinnamon glaze

- ½ cup confectioners' sugar
- 2 tbsp. milk
- ½ tsp. ground cinnamon
- Pinch of salt

Directions

- Set aside the apples, sliced into tiny cubes. If needed, peel them.
- In a large mixing bowl, add the flour, sugar, baking powder, salt, ground cinnamon, and ground nutmeg.
- Combine the milk, butter, egg, and lemon juice in a separate cup.
- Combine the wet and dry ingredients in a mixing bowl and stir only until mixed. Refrigerate the mixture for anywhere from 5 minutes to 2 days after adding the apples (covered).
- Preheat the air fryer to 370° F
- Scoop out apple fritters into 2 tbsp. balls and place a parchment round on the bottom of them. Cook for 6-7 minutes in the air fryer with apple fritters.
- To make the glaze, whisk together the confectioner's sugar, milk, cinnamon, and salt while the chicken is cooking.

BROWNIES

Prep time: 5 min | Cook time: 20 min | Serves: 3

Ingredient

- 4 tbsp. Salted Butter
- ¼ cup White Sugar
- ¼ cup Cocoa Powder
- ½ tsp. Vanilla
- ¼ cup All Purpose / Plain Flour
- ¼ cup Brown Sugar
- 1 Egg
- ⅓ cup Chocolate Chips

Directions

- Preheat air fryer to 350° F. Line 2 mini loaf pans or 1 standard loaf pan with baking paper.
- In a microwave-safe cup, add the butter, brown sugar, white sugar, and cocoa powder. Microwave in 20-second intervals, stirring well after each until butter is fully melted and mixed.
- Whisk in the vanilla extract until fully mixed. Enable for a minute for the bowl to cool slightly.
- Beat in the egg, then stir in the flour until all is well mixed.
- Combine the chocolate chips and fold them in (and the optional chocolate chunks if using).
- Divide the mixture between the pans and bake for 20-25 minutes in the air fryer.
- Allow 10 minutes for the brownies to cool in the loaf pans before transferring to a wire rack to cool fully.

APPLE PIE BOMB

Prep time: 6 min | Cook time: 15-16 min | Serves: 3

Ingredients

- 3 tsp. ground cinnamon
- 1 can Grands canned biscuits
- 1 cup apple pie filling
- ½ cup butter
- ¾ cup sugar

Directions

- Using a knife and a fork, cut the pie filling into small parts.
- Divide the biscuits into two layers and put them on a clean surface. With a rolling pin, roll to a 4-inch circle or flatten with your fingertips.
- Preheat the air fryer to 350° F for 5 minutes.
- Fill each dough ball with filling, then pinch the edges together to seal. Shape the dough into balls.
- Put apple pie bombs about 2 inches apart in an air fryer, cooking in batches depending on how many you can carry.
- Cook, occasionally stirring, for 8 minutes or until golden brown.
- Melt the butter as the first batch bakes.
- Add sugar and cinnamon to a medium mixing bowl.
- Drizzle melted butter over cooked apple pie bombs on all sides, allowing excess to drip off.
- Roll into the cinnamon-sugar mixture and set on a wire rack to cool.
- Continue with the remaining ingredients.
- Serve hot or cold, depending on your choice.

APPLE TURNOVERS

Prep time: 20 min | Cook time: 20 min | Serves: 4

Ingredients

- 1 tsp. Maple Syrup
- 1 tsp. Cinnamon
- 2 Apples skin removed and diced
- 2 tbsp. Water

For turnovers

- 1 Egg, lightly whisked into an egg wash
- 1 sheet Frozen Puff Pastry
- Thickened Cream, whipped

Directions

- Take the puff pastry sheet out of the freezer and let it thaw slightly. Then cut the sheet into four squares and use the egg to brush the edges of each square.
- Fill each puff pastry square with apples, fold the pastry over from corner to corner into a triangle shape and seal the edges with a fork.
- Brush the tops of each turnover with the egg, then put 2 turnovers in the air fryer and cook for 15 minutes at 350° F, or until golden brown. Cook the remaining turnovers in the same manner.
- Serve plain or with a dollop of thickened milk

STRAWBERRY SHORTCAKE

SPANISH CHURROS

Prep time: 10 minutes | Cook time: 10 minutes | Serves 4

Ingredients

- ¾ cup all-purpose flour
- ½ teaspoon baking powder
- ¾ cup water
- 4 tablespoons butter
- 1 tablespoon granulated sugar
- ½ teaspoon vanilla extract
- ½ teaspoon sea salt
- 1 large egg

Directions

- In a mixing bowl, thoroughly combine all ingredients. Place the batter in a piping bag fitted with a large open star tip.
- Pipe the churros into 6-inch long ropes and lower them onto the greased Air Fryer pan.
- Select Bake. Set temperature to 360°F (180°C), and set time to 10 minutes, flipping them halfway through the cooking time.
- Repeat with the remaining batter and serve warm. Enjoy!

Prep time: 10 min | Cook time: 8 min | Serves: 3-4

Ingredients

Strawberry Topping

- Strawberries sliced: 2 cups
- ½ cup confectioner's sugar

Shortcake

- sugar-free whipped cream, as needed
- ⅔ cup water
- ½ cup confectioner's sugar substitute
- ¼ cup butter cold, cube
- 2 cups Carbic

Directions

- Add the strawberries and ½ cup sugar substitute to a big mixing bowl.
- Smash a few strawberries against the side of the bowl to help them start producing juices.
- Set aside, stirring regularly to prevent the strawberries from releasing their juices.
- In a separate bowl, blend the butter and completely add the mixture into the butter.
- Combine the sugar substitute and salt in a mixing bowl.
- Stir in enough water to make a dough.
- Cut dough into 6 biscuits of similar size.
- Place biscuits in the air fryer and air fry (or air crisp) at 400° F for 8 to 9 minutes, or until doughy
- After removing the biscuits from the air fryer, we like to let them rest for 3 minutes.
- Serve upside-down shortcakes with strawberries spooned on top and sugar-free whipped cream on the side, if needed.

Prep time: 10 minutes | Cook time: 13 minutes | Serves 3

Ingredients

- 4 tablespoons all-purpose flour
- 4 tablespoons almond flour
- 1 teaspoon baking powder
- 4 tablespoons honey
- 1 teaspoon pumpkin pie spice blend
- A pinch of Himalayan salt
- ¼ cup milk
- ¼ cup canned pumpkin
- 1 egg, beaten

Directions

- Mix all the ingredients to make the batter. Pour the batter into a lightly oiled baking pan.
- Place the pan in the Air Fryer cooking tray.
- Select Bake. Set temperature to 350°F (180°C), and set time to about 13 minutes or until it is golden brown around the edges.
- Bon appétit!

Prep time: 10 minutes | Cook time: 20 minutes | Serves 4

Ingredients

- ¾ cup all-purpose flour
- ¼ cup butter
- ¼ cup water
- ½ cup full-fat milk
- ¼ teaspoon kosher salt
- A pinch of grated nutmeg
- 3 eggs, beaten

Directions

- In a mixing bowl, thoroughly combine all ingredients. Place the batter in a piping bag fitted with a large open star tip.
- Pipe your crullers into circles and lower them onto the greased Air Fryer pan.
- Select Bake. Set temperature to 360°F (180°C), and set time to 10 minutes, flipping them halfway through the cooking time.

Repeat with the remaining batter and serve immediately. Enjoy!

MEASUREMENT CONVERSION CHART

Volume Equivalents (Dry)

US STANDARD	METRIC (APPROXIMATE)
1/8 teaspoon	0.5 mL
1/4 teaspoon	1 mL
1/2 teaspoon	2 mL
3/4 teaspoon	4 mL
1 teaspoon	5 mL
1 tablespoon	15 mL
1/4 cup	59 mL
1/2 cup	118 mL
3/4 cup	177 mL
1 cup	235 mL
2 cups	475 mL
3 cups	700 mL
4 cups	1 L

Temperatures Equivalents

FAHRENHEIT (F)	CELSIUS(C) (APPROXIMATE)
225 °F	107 °C
250 °F	120 °C
275 °F	135 °C
300 °F	150 °C
325 °F	160 °C
350 °F	180 °C
375 °F	190 °C
400 °F	205 °C
425 °F	220 °C
450 °F	235 °C
475 °F	245 °C
500 °F	260 °C

Volume Equivalents (Liquid)

US STANDARD	US STANDARD (OUNCES)	METRIC (APPROXIMATE)
2 tablespoons	1 fl.oz.	30 mL
1/4 cup	2 fl.oz.	60 mL
1/2 cup	4 fl.oz.	120 mL
1 cup	8 fl.oz.	240 mL
1 1/2 cup	12 fl.oz.	355 mL
2 cups or 1 pint	16 fl.oz.	475 mL
4 cups or 1 quart	32 fl.oz.	1 L
1 gallon	128 fl.oz.	4 L

Weight Equivalents

US STANDARD	METRIC (APPROXIMATE)
1 ounce	28 g
2 ounces	57 g
5 ounces	142 g
10 ounces	284 g
15 ounces	425 g
16 ounces (1 pound)	455 g
1.5 pounds	680 g
2 pounds	907 g

Chicken

INGREDIENT	AMOUNT	PREPARATION	AVG.TIME	TEMP.(ºF)
Tender	1-inch	strips	8 min	360
Breast	4 ounces	Boneless	11 min	380
Wings	2 pounds	/	13 min	380
Thighs	1.5 pounds	Boneless	17 min	380
Drumsticks	2.5 pounds	/	19 min	370
Thighs	2 pounds	Bone-in	21 min	380
Breast	1.25 pounds	Bone-in	24 min	370
Legs	1.75 pounds	Bone-in	30 min	380
Cornish Hen	2 pounds	Whole	32 min	370
Roast Chicken	4 pounds	Whole	55 min	350

Seafood

INGREDIENT	AMOUNT	PREPARATION	AVG.TIME	TEMP.(ºF)
Calamari	8 ounces	/	4 min	400
Shrimp	1 pound	Whole	4 min	400
Lobster Tails	1	Whole	5 min	370
Scallops	1 pound	Whole	6 min	400
Tuna Steak	2 inches	thick	6 min	400
Fish Fillet	8 ounces	/	9 min	400
Swordfish Steak	2 inches	thick	9 min	400
Crab Cakes	1-2 inches	thick	9 min	400
Salmon Fillet	12 ounces	/	10 min	380

Beef

INGREDIENT	AMOUNT	PREPARATION	AVG.TIME	TEMP.(ºF)
Meatballs	2-inch	/	8 min	380
Flank Steak	1.5 pounds	/	11 min	400
Ribeye	8 ounces	Bone-in	11 min	400
Sirloin Steak	12 ounces	/	11 min	400
Burger	4 ounces	/	14 min	370
Filet Mignon	8 ounces	/	16 min	400
London Broil	2 pounds	/	18 min	400
Beef Eye Round	4 pounds	/	45 min	380

Vegetable

INGREDIENT	AMOUNT	PREPARATION	AVG.TIME	TEMP.(^oF)
Brussels Sprouts	/	Halved	15 min	380
Eggplant	1-inch	Chopped	15 min	400
Fennel	/	Quartered	15 min	370
Parsnips	1/2-inch	Chopped	15 min	380
Peppers	1/2-inch	Chopped	15 min	400
Baby Potatoes	1.5 pounds	Small	16 min	400
Cherry Tomatoes	/	Whole	20 min	340
Carrots	/	Whole	20 min	380
Sweet Potato	/	Whole	35 min	380
Beets	/	Whole	40 min	400
Potatoes	/	Whole	40 min	400

Frozen

INGREDIENT	AMOUNT	PREPARATION	AVG.TIME	TEMP.(^oF)
Onion Rings	12 ounces	/	7 min	370 to 400
Mozzarella Sticks	12 ounces	/	7 min	370 to 400
Pot Stickers	10 ounces	/	7 min	370 to 400
Breaded Shrimp	12 ounces	/	9 min	370 to 400
Fish Sticks	10 ounces	/	9 min	370 to 400
Chicken Nuggets	12 ounces	/	10 min	370 to 400
Thin Fries	20 ounces	/	14 min	370 to 400
Fish Fillet	10 ounces	/	14 min	370 to 400
Chicken Wings	6 ounces	Precooked	17 min	370 to 400
Thick Fries	20 ounces	/	17 min	370 to 400

CONCLUSION

The technology of the Breville Smart Oven Air Fryer Pro is exceptionally straightforward. Fried foods get their crunchy feel because warm oil heats meals quickly and evenly onto their face. Oil is a superb heat conductor that aids with simultaneous and fast cooking across each ingredient. For decades' cooks have employed convection ovens to attempt and mimic the effects of cooking or frying the entire surface of the food.

However, the atmosphere never circulates quickly enough to precisely attain that yummy surface most of us enjoy in fried foods. With this mechanism, the atmosphere is spread high levels up to 400°F, into "air fry" any foods like poultry, fish or processors, etc. This technology has altered the entire cooking notion by decreasing the fat by around 80 percent compared to traditional fat skillet. There is also an exhaust fan directly over the cooking room, which offers the meals necessary airflow.

This also contributes to precisely the identical heating reaching every region of the food that's being cooked. This is the only grill and exhaust fan that helps the Smart Oven improve the air continuously to cook wholesome meals without fat. The inner pressure strengthens the temperature, which will be controlled by the exhaust system. Exhaust enthusiast releases filtered additional air to cook the meals in a far healthier way. Smart Oven doesn't have any odor whatsoever, and It's benign, making it easy and environment friendly.

Hopefully, after going through this cookbook and trying out a couple of recipes, **you will get to understand the flexibility and utility of the air fryers**. The use of this kitchen appliance ensures that the making of some of your favorite snacks and meals will be carried out in a stress-free manner without hassling around, which invariably legitimizes its worth and gives you value for your money.

We are so glad you leaped this healthier cooking format with us!

The air fryer truly is not a gadget that should stay on the shelf. Instead, take it out and give it a whirl when you are whipping up one of your tried-and-true recipes or if you are starting to get your feet wet with the air frying method.

Regardless of appliances, recipes, or dietary concerns, we hope you have fun in your kitchen. Between food preparation, cooking time, and then the cleanup, a lot of time is spent in this one room, so it should be as fun as possible.

This is just the start. **There are no limits to working with the air fryer, and we will explore some more recipes as well.** In addition to all the great options that we talked about before, you will find that there are tasty desserts that can make those sweet teeth in no time, and some great sauces and dressing to always be in control over the foods you eat. There are just so many options to choose from that it won't take long before you find a whole bunch of recipes to use, and before you start to wonder why you didn't get the air fryer so much sooner. There are so numerous things to admire about the air fryer, and it becomes an even better tool to use when you have the right recipes in place and can use them. And there are so many fantastic recipes that work well in the air fryer and can get dinner on the table in no time.